PORSCHE 944

Dr. Ing. h.c. Ferry Porsche

PORSCHE 944

Julian MacNamara

ARCO PUBLISHING, INC.
NEW YORK

First published 1984
© Julian MacNamara

Library of Congress Catalog Card Number: 84-70870

ISBN 0-668-06146-4

Published in the USA by Arco Publishing Inc
215 Park Avenue South, New York, N.Y.10003

Filmset by Grange Filmsetting Limited, Birmingham
Printed and bound in Great Britain by
Biddles of Guildford

CONTENTS

Dedicated to my wife with thanks for her help and forebearance
during the writing and research of this book.

Many thanks to Porsche GB Ltd. and the fabulous people in the Press
Department in Zuffenhausen. Also to Andy Rouse and to Tony Dron for
permission to reproduce the picture on page 57.

Part One

The Company and the Men

'We are not only standing at the bier of a great designer, but we are burying with him the heroic epoch of the motor car. Ferdinand Porsche was the last of the great designers, his name was famous all over the world. He belonged with men such as Daimler, Benz, Bugatti and Lancia, names synonymous with the great makes of cars . . . he who rests here before us was blessed by a kind fate which gave the motor car to his creative genius to find complete fulfillment.' The words were those of the German Minister of Transport, Seebohm, spoken in his address to the funeral of Ferdinand Porsche on February 3rd 1951.   Born on 3rd September 1875 the son of Anton Porsche, tinsmith and deputy mayor in the Bohemian town of Maffersdorf, the young Ferdinand Porsche first served notice of exceptional gifts when at the age of fifteen he fitted the family house with electric lighting. Not only did this free Porsche from the previously obstructive attitude of his strict father, it brought him to the attention of the town's biggest business man, one Herr Ginzkey, who in turn used his influence to secure the boy a position with Bela Egger (later Brown Boveri) in Vienna.

Not content with merely finding Porsche a job it would appear that Ginzkey also had a hand in the young man's enrolment at the Vienna Technical University for evening classes. Previously Porsche had been obliged to travel some twenty kilometres each day to the nearest technical school.

The kind fate referred to by Seebohm began to manifest itself almost as soon as Porsche started to interest himself in matters automotive. By a mixture of intelligence and hard work he soon outgrew his responsibilities as an apprentice and having been promoted to head of the service department by the mid eighteen eighties, Porsche patented

The Lohner Porsche electric car shown in the Austrian Pavilion at the Paris Exposition of 1900. Note the electric lighting, rare even on battery powered vehicles in those far off days of acetylene.

an electric drive system utilising hub mounted motors. This patent brought him to the attention of one Joseph Lohner and subsequently Porsche joined the Viennese coachbuilder with the specific task of adapting his design to a car fit to transport the notoriously conservative Emperor Franz Josef.

Little is known of Lohner before his association with Porsche except that he was close to the Emperor and had for many years been official coachbuilder to the house of Hapsburg. The first collaboration of the two men was to bring them fully into the limelight of the contemporary technical world, it was the Lohner Porsche electric car which, with gracious royal patronage, was exhibited in the Austrian Pavilion at the great Paris Exposition of 1900.

Pending the arrival in 1901 of the trend setting Mercedes, there would appear to have been little new in the automotive world at the Exposition and the press seized avidly on the new front wheel drive car. In fact for its day the capabilities of the vehicle were quite remarkable for it could cruise at 37kph (23mph) and the catalogue included a racing version. However it was the hub mounted motors and the front wheel drive which really attracted comment ('the natural location for power insofar as it is from the front which the horse exerts traction', as one eminent German publication expressed it).

The success of the Exposition spurred Porsche to greater things for, having made his name in the press once, the next appearance in print was to be the breaking of the Semmering Hill Climb record for Electricars by some nine and a half minutes: quite a feat considering the mere ten kilometre distance involved. This, however, was 1901 and the year of the epoch making Mercedes. The continuing battle between electricity, the internal combustion engine and steam had taken a positive turn to the advantage of the second and perhaps some dramatic demonstration was needed to retain those customers who couldn't be satisfied by the smoothest transmission currently available coupled with traditional Austro-Hungarian elegance.

Mr. E. W. Hart of Luton taking delivery of a Lohner Porsche car in 1900.

A mixed drive fire tender by Austro Daimler being handed over to the London County Council by Porsche's brother-in-law, Otto Kaes.

The Semmering hillclimb record car with Ferdinand Porsche in control.

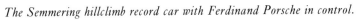

As the motor car became less a local runabout, more a longer distance proposition and touring began to gain international favour, the virtues of the electricar began to be overlooked. Sales began to drop and to counter this trend Porsche developed what must rank as his most important early innovation. Coupling a Daimler petrol engine to a light generator to power the hub motors Porsche produced the first known example of mixed drive. The advantages over the pure electric car were immediately apparent in the extended range and increased power output. The smoothness of the transmission was also preserved although only at a cost of losing the silence of the electricar. The mixture also stressed all its components less heavily than the brutal methods of transmission then current; with the result that a mixed drive car with Porsche at the controls easily outlasted the best of the opposition to win the 1902 Excelberg races in the under 1000kg class.

It is likely that his success in these races led to Porsche gaining the somewhat dubious distinction of being drafted into the Austro-Hungarian army with the exalted rank of Private. In fact he was chosen

The 'C' Train. A further development of mixed drive, the motivating engine drives satellite motors in each of the wagons. This principle was also exploited extremely successfully in the road train (overleaf). Together they made a major contribution to the mobility of the Austro Hungarian forces in the Great War.

The Road Train.

to chauffeur the ill-fated head of the Hapsburg military, Archduke Franz Ferdinand, on annual manoeuvres. That the Archduke was impressed cannot be doubted for a letter still exists to Porsche praising both his services and the vehicle.

By 1905 although retaining a high regard for Porsche's ability Lohner had come to the end of his financial tether. Porsche had by this time taken him into aviation and heavy vehicles and the research and development costs had exhausted him.

Not for the last time colleagues and critics amongst the engineering fraternity were viewing most of Porsche's work as a triumph of engineering over common sense. His carefully thought out drive was effective but complicated and so were many other of his innovations. It was time for a complete change of environment and Porsche was destined to say goodbye to the small but talented and highly devoted team which he had built up at Lohner and move into the thriving Austro Daimler conglomerate where he filled the post left by Paul Daimler who had recently resigned in order to return to the family fold in Stuttgart.

Possibly for the first time in his life Porsche had all the resources he needed to realise his technical ambitions. Almost immediately, although Austria had no aircraft, he embarked on a programme destined to give the central powers aero engine superiority for almost the whole of the great war. By 1913 even the well respected but technically unadventurous company of Beardmore in Britain was manufacturing the water-cooled overhead valve aero engine that Porsche had created specifically for the Parsifal semi rigid airship. Another interesting aero engine design amply presaged the long reliance of the Porsche company on Boxer engines, being a virtual flat four with overhead valves operated by pushrods.

As early as 1902 the Austro Daimler company had built a remarkably reliable and reasonably efficient lorry. With this it had brought about a revolution in the transport policy of the Ministry of War so that the Austro-Hungarian forces were far better equipped than any of the other combatants for the initial war of mobility on the Russian and Italian fronts. As the needs of the military demanded heavier and heavier capacity vehicles so Porsche's mixed drive grew in importance until it was powering the landtrains which could cope with terrain rendered

The Daimler 'Horse', a peacetime agricultural derivative of the tractor Porsche originally designed for varied military duties and the first example of Porsche's life long fascination for the mechanisation of agriculture.

A 1914 electric brougham by Austro Daimler which provided the family with local transport until 1923 with both Ferry and Louise occasionally taking the wheel on the way to school.

impassable to normal mechanised vehicles. These consisted of a truck carrying a generator and feeding multiple self-steering trailers each powered by their own hub mounted electric motors. Other military vehicles for the first world war included an ingenious traction engine with a system of torque-activated 'claws' built into the wheels to give grip in muddy and hilly terrain and the mechanisation of the world's largest siege mortars, the 42cm Skoda which had previously been tied to major railways and permanent installations.

Fascinating as these technically advanced projects were they still did not supplant the love that had grown in Porsche for the motor car and in particular for the racing car. From 1905 until 1908 the mainstay of the Austro Daimler car production was the 'Maja', a fairly conventional four cylinder tourer named after the elder daughter of the Austrian banker whose other daughter had given her name to the Stuttgart produced Mercedes. For once it appears Porsche was content to let well alone, concentrating on the design of an all new 32hp car to be ready for the

1909 season. In fact the car was ready long before the date envisaged and the directors of Austro Daimler felt confident enough to enter a team of three of these cars in that year's Prince Henry Trials, at that time the premier sporting event for any car manufacturer with pretensions towards reliability and high performance.

Although the cars competed well, all three completing the course and being awarded a silver plaque, they were no match for the foreign opposition which in the main consisted of little more than out and out racing machines upon which had been tacked a four seat tonneau type body. Disregarding the congratulations of his fellow directors Porsche set out to design a practical, lightweight tourer which could compete for overall victory in the following year's trials. It seemed a tall order yet the 86hp cars were again ready in good time with eyecatching new style bodywork with a smaller frontal area and cleaner body line than was usual in those days.

So confident was Porsche in the safety and validity of his new design that as one of the three passengers which the rules insisted upon, he took along his wife (legend has it with the newly born Ferry Porsche in arms.) Porsche's confidence was well placed for his new cars swept the board against the most powerful opposition the continent could muster. At one stroke Porsche, the designer, and Austro Daimler, the manufacturer, became bywords to motor enthusiasts across Europe and another clean sweep in the Alpine trials resulted in a booming export order book. A firm belief developed in Porsche's mind that to sell cars it was necessary to show them tested in the field against all opposition and in the full glare of international publicity.

With the coming of the First World War and the amalgamation of Austro Daimler with Skoda, Ferdinand Porsche found many more new projects to occupy him. As well as the land train and the 42cm mortar the lesser 30.5cm mortar had to be fully mechanised, in fact this had been done prior to the commencement of hostilities and probably with a view to making the mortar a viable export to the German Army. Porsche had already made some forays into the field of four wheel drive for all terrain vehicles and here he created a crude looking but mechanically highly sophisticated tractor unit using a large air cooled engine driving all four wheels through a system of bevel gears, the steering to the front wheels being incorporated into this eccentric system.

Eccentric in a different sense was his burning desire to build a helicopter. In fact by 1918 he had solved most of the mechanical problems and by harnessing the lifting capacity of a captive balloon and powering the rotor from a generator on the ground he could have produced a viable and safe artillery observation platform. Certainly it would have been safer than the contemporary kite balloon which, as the Allied airmen became more proficient, and incendiary ammunition grew more efficient, became the cause of the inevitable wastage in trained observers and the men deployed to protect these vital but fragile craft.

With the end of the first world war Austro Daimler faced many severe problems not the least being overmanning and over capacity for the newly reduced size of the market. At the upper end of the car market they quickly assumed a technical supremacy over most contemporaries with an advanced 4.4 litre six cylinder car developing some 60hp. Once more they established a good reputation in such export markets available

In 1916 Austro Daimler had developed a miniature train for use at the front. In service form the engine developed some six horsepower from its flat twin engine. Detuned to give three horsepower it proved the ideal power plant for Ferry Porsche's first 'racing car'.

Ferry's first competition drive.

to them yet it was hardly enough to keep the six thousand strong workforce busy let alone show a profit to a board of directors who were beginning to regard Porsche as an extremely expensive luxury.

For a while Porsche kept his position arguing that a new market needed new products and therefore the company must look towards a smaller car with mass appeal. However his advice fell largely on deaf ears until he mooted an 1100cc ohc sports car suitable for the current voiturette racing class and much more practical to produce and maintain than the full Grand Prix cars of those days.

The little car was duly named Sasha and became an overnight international success when a team of three entered the 1922 Targa Florio taking the first two positions in the voiturette class and seventh in the overall classification. As the cars repeated the story in race after race Porsche drew up plans for two more cars, one was a two litre Grand Prix car and one was a sports car to challenge for honours in the great endurance races. Unfortunately only the Grand Prix car was built and when it crashed due to a material failure in the Italian Grand Prix the writing was well and truly on the wall for Ferdinand Porsche. Thus in early 1923 Porsche accepted an offer from Mercedes in Unterturkheim and leaving his friend and protégé Karl Rabe to take his place at Wiener-Neustadt, took his wife and children to Stuttgart once more to follow in the footsteps of Paul Daimler as technical Director and a full member of the Mercedes board.

11

Supremely successful Sacha with which Porsche attempted to revise the competition fortune of Austro-Daimler immediately following World War One.

It has been said that Ferdinand Porsche conquered Unterturkheim on the mountain roads of Sicily. In this there is quite a lot of truth for when Porsche arrived at Mercedes the design department was about to experience the sort of reversal guaranteed to bring disrepute.

On order from the board a completely new supercharged four cylinder sixteen valve Grand Prix car had been prepared. This, one must remember, was at the time that German workers were carrying home their wages in wheelbarrows and foreign exchange was the most vital and pressing need as the economy staggered disastrously from slump to slump while inflation soared away to undreamed of heights. Thus to debut these cars the company had chosen Indianapolis for the simple reason that not only was America potentially and traditionally a good Mercedes market but even a minor placing at 'The Brickyard' would generate enough precious foreign currency to have made the exercise valid in accounting terms.

Unfortunately the cars were far from ready and all retired in the race after a dismal practice which reduced both mechanics and drivers to near desperation. Porsche was told that it was his priority to make these cars work and for the next nine months he did very little else but work on the Grand Prix cars and supervise the big new villa which he was having built at the Feuerbacher Heide.

At this time Porsche was forty eight and he began to command the respect of the Mercedes personnel by climbing into the Grand Prix cars and testing each modification himself. Even his temper became accepted by the design staff at Unterturkheim as they came to understand a practical and incisive mind which was far too curious about the problems around it to suffer fools or sycophants gladly. Porsche was the type of man who had to be doing something all the while, whether it was tuning one of his engines with a borrowed spanner or correcting the errant lines of a junior draughtsman and he drove no one nearly as hard as he drove himself.

The problem besetting the Grand Prix cars was not straightforward. The complex valve gear was attached to a sophisticated forced induction system and an ill conceived exhaust system. The cars really had to be perfect by the time the public saw them again, for on their performance rested the overseas prestige of the company and on that prestige were built the export sales which might save Mercedes from the fate of countless other German companies. Thus the race chosen was probably the most daunting in the whole pre-war calendar, the Targa Florio. Over four hundred kilometres of the worst roads in Europe with the added risk of over enthusiastic spectators, straying cattle and even the odd local ignoring the race as he pottered home from his favourite trattoria.

Mercedes had first entered the Targa in 1911 and had last won the race in 1921 with a slightly modified 1914 Grand Prix car. To appear here and lose would have been disastrous. Yet on the rock strewn roads against Italian drivers with superb machines and an almost mystical knowledge of the course it was a fraught undertaking to say the least. It was, however, a gamble which paid off. Driving to strict orders Christian Werner just snatched the race from Masetti after Ascari had seized his engine on the last lap. Together Werner and Porsche collected the winner's trophy and set a pattern which was to dominate for the rest of that season.

The next item on Porsche's agenda was a sportscar to rival the international domination of Bentley and Bugatti. Thus was born the

The entry for the new Porsche company in the Stuttgart commercial register dated April 25th 1931.

fabulous SSK and with this car perhaps the greatest Continental driver of all time, the legendary Rudolf Caracciola who first reached public notice by beating Werner in a full Grand Prix specification machine over the Nurburgring in 1927. So impressed was Porsche that he entrusted the new straight eight two litre Grand Prix car to 'Carasch' to be rewarded with a resounding victory in the first ever German Grand Prix. Although never real competition for the Bentleys the SSK was destined to outlast them as it became the SSKL and soldiered on past the bankruptcy which forever emasculated the brilliant British cars. The SSK was Porsche's last real contribution to the charismatic image of the great cars from Unterturkheim, for following the amalgamation of Daimler and Benz he no longer carried any real executive power. Once more his plans for a small car were thwarted by those who felt image more important than mass markets and once more his racing and research budgets were slashed by more establishmentarian colleagues.

Only the pioneer work he had done in adapting the diesel engine for use in trucks remained at Mercedes as a monument to Porsche's term in office there for even the valve location in the later Mercedes Benz cars of the period was an anathema to the logical mind of Porsche. Sadly he repacked his bags and letting the magnificent villa overlooking the city he headed back to Austria where the Steyr Corporation was willing to let him follow his own plans for a two litre production car of a highly advanced specification.

For a short time Porsche was happy among like minded people at Steyr and as well as the two litre car he produced an absolute masterpiece in the Steyr Austria, a straight eight ohv car of 5.3 litres giving some 100bhp. It was also one of the first cars in the world to boast overdrive and its stylish lines made it the star of the 1929 Paris Salon. Just as this was taking place, however, Steyr's bankers went into liquidation pushing the whole of the company into the arms of Austro Daimler. Porsche was once more without a company. At the age of fifty-three it was time for him to start afresh and after much thought he decided that the independent route was the most attractive; thus at last he bade goodbye to the strait-jacket of business accountancy and headed back to his villa in Stuttgart determined to forge a new dynasty.

The name plate which went up over the premises in Zuffenhausen modestly read just, 'Dr.Ing.h.c. F. Porsche KG' and it is some measure of the great man's charisma that in those straitened times he was able to attract the very finest of talents to him in this new venture. From Austro Daimler he brought Karl Rabe who had sorted out the development problems on the torque activated 'claws' for Porsche's gun towing tractor whilst from the other companies he had been associated with men of the calibre of Erwin Kommenda. Even the fanatically pro Daimler Benz chief of Mercedes Benz racing operations Neubaur was later to admit in his autobiography that he had been tempted to rejoin the man he had originally followed from Wiener Neustadt to Stuttgart.

Almost from the time he started his own company the economic tide in Germany began to turn to the advantage of the new venture. First Zundapp then DKW, Wanderer and NSU all came to consult at the new design bureau although the very reason which sent them thither to find

15

An early commission was the Type 9 Zundapp.

talent to commence car production, which was the steadily improving financial climate, actually prevented Zundapp and NSU from commencing production, for the upturn in the demand for motorcycles took the total available production space.

With a steady throughput of both detail and full project design work Porsche looked toward his other inspirations which had lain dormant in the years spent in the larger organisations and eventually in 1933 managed to solve the technical problems preventing the widespread application of torsion bar suspension. At this point the work literally flooded in as such diverse customers as General Motors and Morris joined the queue for the latest, safest and most economical suspension system. At last financial success had crowned the academic and corporate success which had seen Ferdinand Porsche gain his doctorate in 1918 for work in the field of aviation and then join the central boards of the succession of companies in which he found himself.

There can really be no doubt that the solution of the problems inherent in the manufacture of the torsion bar system was the greatest commercial achievement of Ferdinand Porsche, but equally valid are the

Prototype design for Wanderer in which the beginnings of the VW can just be discerned.

The NSU Type 32 clearly points the way that the Porsche was due to follow in the development of the Volkswagen. Unfortunately the company was unable to put the car into production.

two immediate avenues in which the man himself chose to pursue the development of his brainchild.

Although the directors of NSU at Neckarsulm had been unable to put into production Porsche's type 32, his grasp of the principles of marketing and design had impressed them enough that on formation of the Auto Union they were in a fine position to recommend the appointment to the newly formed corporation of Professor Porsche in the capacity of designer for the proposed racing programme which the newly elected National Socialist party was co-sponsoring. Although opinions differ as to the actual date that the corporation first approached Porsche there can be little doubt that the maestro was already working on such a project on his own initiative for in 1934 the sensational mid engined 'Silver Fish' appeared and the resultant humiliation of all the proudest international motor racing names is now history.

So impressed was the new Chancellor that he appointed Porsche to the task of seeing his pet dream become reality. At the Autoshow in Frankfurt in 1935 Hitler announced to a rapturous population and a cynical automotive industry the birth of the Volkswagon under the sole direction of 'the brilliant automotive designer Herr Professor Porsche.' Not only was Porsche to design the car but Porsche was also to design the fabulous and massive new factory and the town that would surround it for the express purpose of providing the German people with means of

The chassis of the 1934 Auto Union. The layout clearly foreshadows today's racers.

breaking down the obvious class barrier of superior middle class mobility. To the man who had begged for some thirteen years to create a car for the masses such an assignment was a personal and professional triumph of the highest magnitude and he set out to meet it in the highest of spirits as his Grand Prix cars set out to sell the new reawakened Germany on the world's race tracks.

Part of the brief which Hitler had given Porsche was that the new car was to cost less than one thousand Reichsmarks, the equivalent in those days of some four hundred US dollars. Also the rest of the German motor industry was to cooperate with the new venture in providing both expertise and in some cases more practical help in the form of personnel secondment and material availability. In effect the rest of the industry feeling itself under threat started a 'knocking' campaign against the new venture with the cruellest cut of all coming from Daimler Benz whose rear engined 130 model was based firmly upon all the principles for which Porsche was forced to leave, although the engine was an inline water-cooled four rather than the boxer flat four that Porsche and his

19

3 Weltrekorde für Deutschland

DER AUTO UNION RENNWAGEN

stellte am 6. III. 34 auf der Avus bei Berlin folgende neue Weltbestzeiten auf:

für 100 MEILEN ..... 216,869 KILOMETER
für 200 KILOMETER... 217,085 KILOMETER
in 1 STUNDE ..... 217,106.79 km

Both as a marketing tool of the newly formed Auto Union and as a standard bearer for the new National Socialist Germany the racing car became a fine instrument of propaganda.

20

few forward-looking contemporaries such as Ledwinka propounded.

Perhaps a lesser man than Porsche would have become bitter under the welter of bureaucratic meddling and entrenched prejudice which conspired to hold back the development of the car. (Another factor in the slowness of the car's transition from prototype to production was the demand from the Reichschancellor that the project should be financed in the greatest measure by the pre-comitted savings of those for whom the car was eventually intended, in other words the German workers.) Problems beset the project on all sides and yet the father of the VW took all in his stride and kept his dedicated team to the task allotted with a mixture of kind encouragement and selfless example.

The Volkswagon development period was also the time for the alignment of all the family talents beneath the roof of the design studio as it allowed Ferry Porsche to return from his stay at NSU, where he had been liaising upon the type 32 project, to take up the reins on the Auto Union racing car as his father spent more of his time at the emerging VW headquarters at Wolfsburg.

Ferry Porsche at the wheel of one of the pre-production series Volkswagen prototypes.

21

A driver of no mean ability, Ferry Porsche had been carefully prepared from the cradle onward to inherit the mantle of Porsche senior. From the time he could walk the boy became a familiar figure to his father's workmates at Austro Daimler as he followed the great man about his daily business. His first car was even built for him by the staff of the Austro Daimler company, a pedal replica of the Prince Henry model which he took delivery of on his fourth birthday in September 1909.

With the advent of school both he and his sister Louise became familiar figures in the area as they occasionally took the wheel of the family's Lohner electric brougham on their daily journeys so that at Christmas 1919 Porsche had no qualms in handing his excited son a miniature two cylinder replica of the forthcoming Sasha. Luckily for the younger Porsche the local constabulary were well conversant with his father's standing both at Austro Daimler and in the community generally for the young man saw no reason to follow the counsel of his father and restrict his motoring to the roads on the estate. Indeed, stories began to circulate of twenty mile trips in the little car with a school friend as 'riding mechanic'. At this point the elder Porsche found a means of keeping his wayward son in order by allowing him the privilege of driving one of the works Sashas on the company roads thus making sure he was close to hand and under adequate supervision.

In 1928 having matriculated from high school Ferry went as an apprentice to the electrical giant Bosch. In the year that he spent here he began to take steps toward becoming a racing driver with the purchase of a BMW 500 motorcycle. With scant regard for his son's feelings Ferdinand Porsche confiscated the machine but then as if in moderation brought his son into his own company as a junior draughtsman and allowed him to do much of the test driving on the new Wanderer two litre, a car which was to bring Ferry some success in forest rallies and trials. In one such rally, the Hartz, the young Porsche actually managed to beat the immortal Bernt Rosmeyer when he won his class, a feat repeated on the Baden-Baden. However with the the words, 'It is his job to design them, not to race them,' his father put an end to the young man's dreams of international stardom.

Perhaps a factor which played some part in Ferry's acceptance of his father's dictates was his forthcoming marriage, for just a few months after the announcement of the VW programme Ferry settled down to produce four sons each in turn to enter the family company and each to become equal members in one of the most exclusive business 'clubs' in the world, the Porsche Shareholders. His sister was also in the process of marriage by this time and once more the good fortune which seems to have characterised the house of Porsche must have smiled. For in the figure of Anton Piech she brought into the family circle one of the great motivators in the present German motor industry and a man with all the stamina and flair needed to steer the commercial fortunes of the company through the tumultuous events which awaited it.

By 1937 the first pre-production batch of Volkswagens were ready and the car became more than a dream. Suddenly the German worker could see his car and the orders began to flood in, each worker being provided with a card upon which he could stick a stamp purchased through his local party representative, towards the eventual price of his own personal KdF (Strength through Joy) car. The various practical derivatives such as the small utility for the postal services and the Kubelwagen for the military and the farmers were taking shape and

A model of the proposed Type 114 Volkswagen based prototype of 1938.

This project for Mercedes Benz was built specifically to attack the World Land Speed Record in 1939. The war intervened. The car resides today in the Mercedes Museum in Stuttgart.

Ferdinand Porsche approached the Arbietsfront for permission to build a sports car based on the VW floor pan and mechanicals.

At first the request was treated with a certain amount of contempt by the gauleiters of the industry; a sports car, in bureaucratic opinion, not being a vehicle for the masses. However, events were in train which would soon cause them to hastily reappraise the situation.

Although politically Italy and Germany were very closely aligned the two countries were fighting bitterly for prestige upon the race tracks of the world with the battle weighted heavily in favour of the Germans on the Grand Prix front. So complete was the Teutonic domination that with the exception of the 1500cc voiturette class where honours were more or less evenly divided between the British ERA and the Italian Alfettas and Maseratis that long distance road races were beginning to take over the prestige of the Grand Prix in many people's eyes.

With the exception of the superb BMW 327 and 328 Germany was somewhat lacking in endurance racing potential. France could boast the magnificent Talbots, Bugattis and Delahayes. Italy could claim some of the best all-round machinery in any classes thanks once again to Alfa

Romeo and Maserati concerns, whilst Britain was once again dominating sports car racing through such names as Lagonda, Fraser Nash, SS Jaguar, Singer and Riley, the latter in the smaller capacity classes.

It was with this scenario that the Berlin-Rome-Berlin race was mooted and, in the early months of 1939 officially included in the international calendar as the Berlin-Rome race for Autumn 1939. The Arbietsfront now embraced the idea of a VW based sportscar with fervour, for after all, Adolf Hitler himself was a passionate devotee of motor racing and the Volkswagen was his personal pet project.

The Porsche design team had already made detailed drawings of three possible VW based cars in September 1938. All mid engined, some with two seats, one with three, two with standard but slightly tuned VW engines and one with supercharging. The Type 64 VW was in fact, literally an extensively revised version of these plans somewhat updated by draughtsman Karl Frohlich to maximise the aerodynamics in view of the fact that the race was to take advantage of the new Berlin to Munich autobahn for part of the route.

The sole surviving Berlin – Rome car pictured outside the Porsche family villa at Feurbacher Heide.

Three proto types of the car were built bearing the chassis type 60 K 10. All were powered by a standard VW powerplant tuned to give some 40bhp and the driver sat centrally with the passenger seated somewhat offset to his right further back. Unfortunately the war intervened at this point and the proposed race never took place but one prototype was destined to survive both the war and the mindless vandalism of the occupying Americans and is now in private hands in Austria. A recognisable forerunner of the cars to come.

Once more Porsche's proximity to a head of state assured that much Government and war effort work found its way to the Stuttgart design offices. Porsche technicians gave service on every technical front from aviation to ballistics. Once again however Porsche's somewhat over engineered solutions to design problems tended to alienate the military from buying his projects, his super tank design being passed over in favour of Willi Henschel's for instance, but even so the war years proved quite profitable and in terms of pure research extremely fruitful.

With the war situation worsening and daily bombings of both Stuttgart and Wolfsburg taking place the decision was taken in 1944 to safeguard the Porsche factory by relocating it. The place chosen by the ministry concerned was deep in Czechoslovakia and as such too close to the Russian front for the liking of the Porsche family. Using all his powers of persuasion and every high ranking contact available Ferry managed to get the order transferred to Gmund in Austria.

With the inevitable collapse of social structure and the debasing of the currency which followed the war the company had to begin once more its search for both identity and work. At first the workforce made a token living from repairing the thousands of broken down vehicles left from the devastation. The Volkswagen especially became a favourite of the local American occupation forces and who better than the designer to keep them going?

Slowly the company began to rebuild as staff trickled back from the various fronts and refugee centres. Porsche was still an internationally famous name and there was still work to be done in the world motor industry. The invitation, when it came, to travel to France in order to help solve the more glaring design problems with the proposed Renault 4 must have seemed like the dawn of a new day to the war weary Ferdinand Porsche.

At first all was well. The design staff at Renault were courteous and helpful to the visiting genius and the time was right for the rebirth of the newly nationalised French giant with its fine little peoples car. Unfortunately a certain rival within the French motor industry whose own record during the war years was extremely suspect seized on the employment of Porsche by the state owned giant to make political capital, claiming that the firm of Porsche had used slave labour under the aegis of the Nazi government during the war years.

With little ceremony Ferdinand and Ferry were thrown into jail and the family's estates impounded by the French occupation forces. Once more it was left to Ferry to use all his resources in guile and tact to save the situation, firstly by obtaining his own freedom and the restitution of the family estate at Zell Am See and secondly by raising the ransom demanded by the French for his father's release.

Fearing for the health and even the life of his father, Ferry returned to Gmund where the British had now taken over from the Americans and appointed Karl Rabe to run the business. Immediately the idea of

Ferdinand Porsche with Ferry working in the engine department at Gmünd.

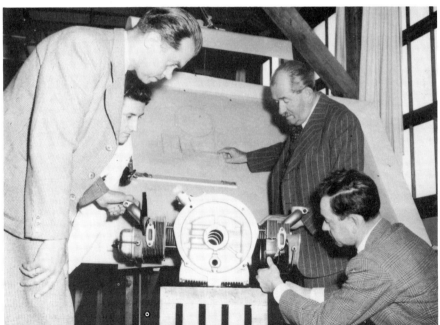

building cars returned to Ferry as the best means of raising the capital
needed to ransom his father. The first project to come into the new
design offices was the commission from Italian industrialist Piero Dusio
for the Cisitalia Grand Prix car. It was a start. On July 17th 1947 the
design of a new VW based sports car started under the design number
356. It was to be a tubular space frame construction with a mid mounted
largely standard VW power plant and what the factory described
somewhat euphemistically as an 'occasional roof'. Once more Ferry was
called upon to provide the funds to build the car, so armed with
drawings, specifications and a list of addresses of well wishers and
acquaintances, mainly in Switzerland, he set out to pre-sell the first car
ever to bear the name Porsche.

The 356 was soon to become the keystone of the family's business
survival but at the outset it was very much a matter of desperation that
brought the car into being. The war wasted expanses of Europe were
hardly the likely market for anything so reminiscent of the balmy days of
the thirties as a luxury two seater. The Swiss franc and the Swedish
krona were really the only currencies which had survived in anything

An early Cabriolet being collected by the proud owner at Gmünd.

like reasonable shape thus it was no surprise that the first 356 was duly sold to one of the two Swiss businessmen who had funded Ferry, one Mr. R. Von Senger of Zurich.

Giving 40bhp from an almost standard 1131cc Volkswagen power plant the first 356 was avidly seized by the respected Swiss journal *Automobile Revue* as soon as it was delivered in March 1948. The aluminium bodywork helped keep the weight down to some 596kg with a full tank and the mid engine obviously helped the handling somewhat for the magazine commented in its road test that it displayed grip around the difficult Bremgarten circuit.

Although the car amply fulfilled all that could be desired of it as far as its road behaviour was concerned it left a lot to be attended to in terms of a marketable commodity. Space was needed for luggage and for the occasional third or fourth passenger. The engine had to be serviceable with a minimum of expertise and tooling. The space frame was far too expensive in terms of man hours even for that work starved time and more standardisation with the current 'Beetle' was necessary due to the agreement signed between the two companies which in effect allied their

Ferdinand Porsche with an early Cabriolet Gmünd 1948.

distribution agreements in return for the ongoing involvement of Porsche in VW development.

The second car from Gmund was very much a product of this rational thinking. The engine had returned to the position it occupied in VW, the space frame had made way for a pressed steel floor pan strengthened by the novel incorporation of box section side members. The coupé body was also recognisably different from the first car but still very much a product of the Porsche school of thought. Simultaneously a drophead was built which gave the fledgling concern another product with which to woo the straitened market.

By this time Ferdinand Porsche had been ransomed from the French and although his health never recovered he became a father figure in the little factory in the Austrian hills. In all some forty-six cars were built by the Gmund factory, each one with aluminium bodywork hand beaten over wooden stretchers in the traditional way. Business was so hectic that cars had been assembled not only by the design and finishing staff in Gmund but also by Tatra and Kastenhofer in Vienna.

The first gathering of Porsche owners at Schloss Solitude on September 3rd 1950, the occasion of Ferdinand Porsche's seventy-fifth birthday.

Of these early cars some fifteen were taken by the Swedish giant Scania Vabis who had taken the Porsche agency for that country. Many of the others were taken by racers who used the superior power to weight and better braking characteristics than the subsequent steel built Stuttgart products.

With the exhibition of a 356 at the Geneva show in 1949 came the welcome news that the Americans were relinquishing their hold on the company's factory in Stuttgart. By this time the Swiss coachbuilder Beutler had joined the catalogue of outside coachbuilders building to the order and under the name of Porsche. Slowly the company made the transition back to the capital Wurttemburg.

At first the company was forced to rent production space from the bodybuilding firm of Reutter at the nominal rent of 1Dm per metre, however, by the spring of 1950 production was well under way and the official participation of the company in the following year's Le Mans was under discussion as a result of the French importer, one M. Veuillet, making a direct offer to Ferdinand Porsche at the Paris Salon.

The car duly took first in class in 1951 just two months after the delivery of the five hundredth customer car from Reutters. The cars had already shown well in several events but it was this victory at Le Mans which really took the car from the pages of the central European trade journals into the consciousness of the motoring world in general. Some three months later the one thousandth car left the factory and 1951 closed with 1,103 cars built by a staff of 214 at a turnover of 12,500,000 Dm.

On Ferdinand Porsche's seventy-fifth birthday, September 3rd 1950, a gathering of Porsche owners convened at Schloss Solitude. They were already an international and wealthy group but the really exciting aspect of the meeting was just how many of these Porsche owners were prepared to travel to join the family at this early time in the car's history.

Sadly some five months later Ferdinand Porsche died but, in the meantime much had happened to the fledgling concern. With the 356 established by its success at Le Mans the time was coming when a new car had to be developed to keep up with the pace of international competition. Even on its own home territory, competing against largely pre-war or modified VW powered specials, the steel bodied 356 was hardly a natural front runner.

31

The Glockler car which dominated the German hillclimb championships for three years before the factory took the project in house to create the immortal series of 'spiders'.

Realising this a Porsche agent from Frankfurt decided to do something to rectify the situation. Taking the basics of the 356 he clothed it in a streamlined, low slung body made entirely of aluminium and leaving driver protection to the smallest possible aero tyre screen and a half tonneau created what was for the day a highly effective and fairly advanced racing car.

The Glockler Porsche, as the car became known after its originator was an immediate success. The first car was built by Wiederhausen in Frankfurt and boasted an 1100cc engine with 58bhp to move an all up weight of 450kg. Using the car to maximum advantage, where power to weight and good handling outweighed sheer performance Hermann Kathrein won the 1100cc class in the German hillclimb championship in 1951. The feat was duplicated in the same car the next year by Hans Brendel and the factory began to use the car as a basis for the vehicle which was to really shoot the competition side of the firm into the public eye.

The Spyder which was to grow from the Glockler Porsche was to influence a whole generation of Americans. The car was powered by the four cam engine designed by Dr. Fuhrmann and bearing the factory design number 547. It formed a logical chain in a marketing progression in the United States which began with a series of fifteen specially built

'American Roadsters', with lowered screens and more slippery looking bodywork which were completed in 1952 and were in reality the forebears of the famous Speedster.

These cars saved some 60kg over the normal 356, which had by this time evolved into a recognisably better machine with a choice of power plants ranging from 1100cc to 1500cc. It still did not turn the coupé into a car which could have overall winning potential in the tough world of US sports car club racing. The obvious course to Porsche was to bring the Glockler car in house, which it did in 1952, and build it as a factory racer while making it available to a few selected customers.

In 1953 Helm Glockler debuted the new car with a fairly standard pushrod based 1500S engine in the Eifel Race. The run was satisfactory and the factory felt confident enough to enter two similar vehicles at that year's Le Mans. These shared the 1500cc class honours crossing the line side by side after an exemplary 24 hours. The next step was to give the car even more power, hence the Fuhrmann engine, and take the project to the private owners in the USA. It was one of these owners, a young film star looking for a more race-worthy mount than his obsolete MG

The 551 RS Spyder of 1954 seen here at Zuffenhausen.

Front and rear views of the 1952 American Roadster which formed the basis for the Speedster.

TC who was to give the car the publicity which forever established the name and the car with the US public.

Driving at sunset in the Nevada desert James Dean was unable to avoid a car which had taken to the wrong side of the road whilst negotiating a cross road. His death became front page news and as always the power and maximum speed of the car were exaggerated by the press. Souvenir hunters wrenched pieces off the car's bodywork with their bare hands; the youth of Europe and America mourned, but the Porsche was the car to aspire to, and if one couldn't have the fabulous Spyder any Porsche would do.

By this time, 1955, the 356 had become the 356A and a spread of engines bearing only the vaguest resemblance to the humble VW were available from the 1300 Damen to the 1600 Carrera. Porsche had taken

The 356A first appeared in 1955 complete with curved windscreen, refashioned interior, chrome and rubber inserts in the bumpers and side trims and a host of other detail improvements. By this time most of the original VW parts had been discarded but until the end of its model life the 356 was generally thought of as a VW 'special' by non Porsche enthusiasts. Pictured here is a rare right hand drive British specification car.

Probably the most sought after of all the early road going Porsches, the classic 1955 Speedster.

class honours in just about every major international sports car event plus the Monte Carlo Rally and had caused a sensation with overall victory in the gruelling Carrera Panamerica, hence the name of the prestigeous and powerful top of the range car.

In 1956 the firm reached its silver jubilee and celebrated the production of its ten thousandth vehicle, a 356A coupé. At this point the factory began to consider a model to replace the 356. The original plant, known in the company as factory number one, was finally released by the US occupation forces and the offspring of both Ferry Porsche and his sister Louise Piech were beginning to be the third generation to take up positions within the firm. As well as Reutters, who were building bodyshells at the rate of twenty-five per day, the company had commissioned Drauz of Heilbron to build the cabriolets which became known hence forth as D Types. On the motor sport front the year was crowned by Maglioli taking an almost unbelievable overall victory in the Targa Florio with the latest 130bhp 550A Spyder.

In 1957 EMW who had been Porsche's closest international competition were withdrawn from international racing by the East German government, leaving the factory to take what amounted to a clean sweep at class level in racing world wide. A new version of the Spyder was under preparation for sale to private entrants. It emerged in 1958, even lower and sleeker and offering in ex-factory trim some

142bhp at 7,500rpm. It was known as the RS-K and driven by the brilliant pairing of Stirling Moss and Jean Behra it vied with the 3 litre Ferraris at the top level of international motorsport giving Porsche second overall in that year's World Championship for Makes. A supreme achievement for a car conceding some 1400cc to the opposition.

1958 also saw the company enter Formula Two with a single seater of mid-engined design but against the might of the likes of Lotus, Cooper, Ferrari and the host of well organised privateers who ran the mainly British cars the best they could manage was a single victory at Rheims. Nonetheless it was an auspicious debut into the single seater formulas.

1959 saw the advent of the much revised and restyled 356B. At last the interior of the car was brought into line with the prevailing standards of comfort. The last vestiges of the VW heritage could well be said to have been smothered, for a constant search for performance had changed almost every component on the car. Even so the 356 was definitely nearing the end of its model life span and Ferry Porsche detailed the qualities needed in its successor thus: 'interior larger than a 356 and

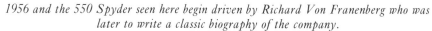

1956 and the 550 Spyder seen here begin driven by Richard Von Franenberg who was later to write a classic biography of the company.

By 1959 sleeker bodywork and more powerful engines characterised the 356B. As can be seen the most noticeable cosmetic changes lie in the shape and location of the bumpers, the larger windscreen and the redesigned hood trim.

large enough to carry golf clubs; six cylinder engine with overhead camshafts and air cooling; four and five speed gearbox options; Macpherson strut front suspension; disc brakes on all four wheels; acceleration and top speed values equal to the Carrera two; better comfort and lower noise levels than the 356.'

Certain parameters of the car, for instance the wheelbase and the rear location for the engine, were set from the start, also it was Ferry Porsche's stated wish that the car be immediately recognisable as the linear descendant of the 356. At the end of the day the new project was given the internal design project number of 901. The job of styling the car went to Ferry's son Ferdinand (known always in the plant by the nick name 'Butzi') and his nephew Ferdinand Piech (whose father Anton had been interned by the French with Professor Porsche) was given detail design responsibility on the mechanical side.

At this stage in the company's evolution the need for product development facilities including a test track began to be felt. Land in Stuttgart being at a premium the decision was taken to split these from the main factory complex and relocate them some thirty minutes away on land owned by the family at Weissach. By 1960 the test track had been laid and soon Helmuth Bott was to move his staff to wooden barrack hut type accommodation. By this time the basis of the company's finance was almost equally gathered from development work for other manufacturers and the products, including a range of agricultural tractors, marketed directly under the name of Porsche.

In the reorganisations which attended the opening of the sixties the tractors were deemed of no further importance and the designs and plant sold to a competitor. Thus the firm was left to introduce a further updated 356, designated 356C, and concentrate the huge weight of its available talent on the introduction of the new car.

Meanwhile on the racing front the redoubtable Spyders were nearing the end of their racing competitiveness. Carlo Abarth, the Italian genius who specialised in tuning Fiats and had worked with Ferry on the ill fated Cisitalia project was approached by the factory to build a new Carrera around the newly developed two litre 180bhp racing engine then under completion.

This car which made its debut in 1960 was to be one of the most

When the capacity for Formula One racing was reduced to 1.5 Litres in 1961 Porsche entered the fray. Here Dan Gurney is seen giving the company its only Grand Prix victory in the 1962 French Grand Prix.

beautiful cars the company had ever produced, a perfect marriage of German engineering and Italian handling and style. Although not an all out prototype racer the car was to take many honours in production sports car events and with its aerodynamically efficient shape it gave added impetus to the Porsche engineers to produce the range of racing cars destined eventually to take the company to the World Championship for Makes and keep it there for the best part of two decades.

In 1961 the four cylinder engine was superseded in the works prototypes by an engine of eight cylinders with four overhead cams liberating a genuine 210bhp. To a certain extent the engine was introduced before it had finished its full development term and disappointing showings resulted in the first few races. The next two seasons proved frustrating for the factory team because a formula one project was under way, as well as the new car which was scheduled for introduction in 1964, the sports prototypes could not be afforded the full attention of the factory.

To say that the involvement of the factory in Formula One was somewhat abortive is to ignore that it was the impetus of this type of racing which created the need for the flat eight engine and paved the way for the development of the 904. Also it provided one Formula One victory from two season's racing, a ratio some far better funded and more experienced teams have occasionally failed to emulate. The 904 with its two litre version of the engine began development at just the time of the Formula One team's disbandment using personnel who had gained experience in this the most competitive of all racing, thus the seemingly wasted efforts of 1960, 1961 and 1962 were fully justified by the long term success of their offspring.

As the company entered 1963 the last version of the 356 was under preparation for announcement. The 356C was to be the epitome of the line of cars started in those far off days in Carinthia. Since 1960 a full two litre engine had been on offer to the general public and the car had benefitted greatly from a host of detail changes in such areas as the hoods of the cabrios and the attention to the lights, bumpers and general refinement of lines, larger rear window, deeper dash panels and twin rear air intake panels.

The real work of the factory at this time, however, was to ready the all new car for launch the following year. It is true to say, in fact, that the whole of the company's future strategy lay in the events leading up to the launch of the 901, or as it was renamed after an objection from Peugeot who held the rights to all production car nomenclature numbers incorporating the central 0, the 911. Originally the plan was to build the 356C and the 911 side by side at Zuffenhausen with the 911 scheduled to start at only some five units per week and with the cool reaction of both press and Porsche owners to the 1964 launch this was felt by many in the company to represent a realistic estimate of the car's potential. The sports car buying public, however, decided differently.

Looking at the luke-warm press which greeted the car it seems incredible that some twenty years ago the Porsche traditionalists were digging in their heels and claiming that a 'proper' Porsche had only four cylinders and lamenting the solid look of the 356 whilst criticising the handling foibles of a car which although not yet perfect was certainly easier to drive than the models which ran before it. It seems there is always an element of the conservative in the followers of any particular

1963, the 911 makes its debut with the last 356C model range in the background.

marque who will damn the new in favour of the old. Perhaps that is why the current range of magazines which deal with classic performance motor cars sell so well. Even so the firm of Porsche seems to have attracted these followers in their droves long before the cars became collectors' items.

As introduced the flat six engine of the 911 gave some 130bhp at 6200rpm. Its standard equipment featured gadgets which although commonplace now were almost unique then such as electric windscreen wash and wipe, heated rear screen and laminated windscreen, asymmetrically dipping lights, reversing lights, and fog lights. The flat six engine with single ohc per bank of three cylinders was fed by six Solex 40 PJ carburettors, self-adjusting drive chains to the camshafts cut down noise and maintenance costs while the Biral casting of the cylinders allowed greater engine life with less weight than any traditional method. The combustion chambers were hemispherical with the valves in a V position allowing not only good initial breathing but

Bjorn Waldegaard in 1969 Monte Carlo Rally. The 911 won three years running with Vic Elford taking the honours in 1968, Waldegaard in 1969 and 1970. In 1978 the 911 was to win the event yet again, second place was gained in 1981.

Ferry Porsche reclining on a 911. This shot was issued as a postcard by the Publicity department in Zuffenhausen.

also plenty of latitude for further enhancing the power output without drastically restructuring the heads which were individually cast.

From a practical point of view the car offered more usable interior space per metre of exterior space than almost any other vehicle then currently on the road. The package was further enhanced by a price of 21,900 Dm, a price which made it more than competitive with any other vehicle then offering similar performance.

So successful was the car in the market place that the last 356C, a cabriolet, left the works less than a year after the 911 was launched. In all 76,302 examples of the car, which had grown almost organically from the drawing boards in Gmund, had taken to the world's highways. They had left a legacy of reliable high speed motoring which even if it was never quite as exotic in image as say a Ferrari GTO or a Jaguar E Type, had brought a new sense of fun to many searching for the flavour of those cars without the crippling costs and thoroughbred temperamentality.

As customer acceptance demanded more of the 911 so the factory provided more. The quirks in the handling were gradually eliminated, a Targa version with removeable top was announced in 1965 along with the 912, obviously a traditionalist's car for it was powered by the trusty flat four 1600cc engine whilst offering a more basic or less luxurious 911 body. While this happened the 904 and its immediate successor the 906 were taking full advantage of the host of private entrants who were queueing to buy them in whittling away Porsche's competitors' advantage in the World Championships for makes.

The list price of a 906 fitted with the six cylinder 901 engine with fuel injection, 904 suspension and with new aerodynamic fibre glass bodywork over a beautifully wrought tubular space frame was some 45,000 Dm. Some fifty two of these cars were built to qualify for the GT class in endurance racing and another fifteen for the prototype class with either the flat four or flat eight pure racing engines. While still not outright winners at the very highest echelons of the sport these cars swept all before them in the German hillclimbs and in their class in the various European sportscar championships.

At the 1967 Targa Florio the new 910, a further development of these cars, took the first three places, the winning car running with a new fuel injected version of the eight cylinder engine which had been overbored to 2.2 litres. Now the writing was well and truly on the wall that the

'Butzi' Porsche at the wheel of the beautiful epoch-making 906.

A cutaway of the 906 with flat four two litre engine.

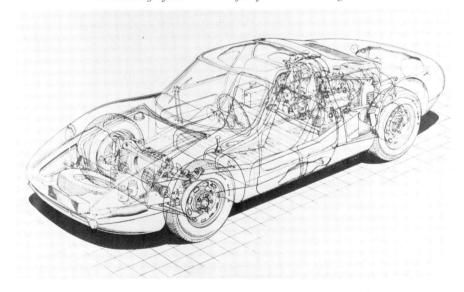

Stuttgart company was earnestly trying for the coveted World Championship for Makes. Later that season a new car appeared, outwardly a development of the 910 but with a different body; from this was to develop one of Porsche's greatest racing cars.

In April 1968 in response to the FIA limiting engine size in the prototype class for endurance racing, Porsche unveiled a brand new eight cylinder 3 litre racing engine designed by Dipl Ing Hans Mezger. The engine was installed in a modified 907 chassis which had been somewhat lengthened. This was the first of the fabulous 908's, a car destined to be competitive in international racing right up until the early 1980's. The car started its career auspiciously with a win in its third outing at the Nurburgring 1000 Kilometres. After a distinguished year's racing, including a full sweep of the first three places at the Brands

The fearsome 917 seen here at Brands Hatch in the livery of the Gulf sponsored John Wyer team who with Porsche Salzburg (later Martini Porsche) were to keep the beast at the forefront of international racing for three years, in the process giving Porsche the World Championship for Makes three years running.

Hatch 1000, they were either sold to privateers or put into service to back up the even more legendary car which was just then being readied in Zuffenhausen, the fearsomely powerful five litre 917.

As public interest followed the exploits of the racers so the 911 went from strength to strength. In 1966 the 911S arrived to a rapturous welcome from the international press, giving 160bhp and overcoming all prejudice with its secure handling and comfortable interior. For those who needed something more sedate the following year saw the introduction of the 911T with 110bhp but substantially improved economy with little loss on overall touring performance. To slot neatly between these models the 911L was added with ostensibly the same bodyshell and trim as the 'S' but a less powerful engine giving 130bhp.

In 1969 the overt link with VW resurfaced with the announcement that a new mid-engined car powered by either a Porsche six cylinder engine or a VW flat four would shortly be available. The new car bore the type number 914 with the suffix of 4 or 6 depending on the power plant. Developed as a joint venture to give VW a market leader in the US the 914 never achieved the success its early reception should have ensured for it. With its mid-engined layout and unique styling the car failed to gain the reception from the conservative lower end of the sports car market which it deserved. As a rule buyers tended to think it too expensive and too difficult to maintain although when marketed as a Porsche in the USA acceptance was far higher than as a VW Porsche in most European territories.

The evolution of the 911 was once again in evidence as a need to prepare for in-coming US emission legislation. The result was to give more torque and smoothness to the European car as well as an average increase of some 10bhp across the range (in the case of the 911S 170bhp to 180bhp at 6500rpm). Economy was unaffected.

The big event of 1969 though, came at the Geneva Salon in March when the company announced the availability of the 917. With a price tag of 140,000 Dm and a 4.5 litre largely built from the components of the 908 mated to a chassis largely derived from the same car the car looked mean and later in the year its drivers confirmed that it was mean.

The regulations for homologation into the World Championship for Makes called for a minimum of twenty-five cars of the same type to be built. From basic design go ahead in late July 1968 to a line of some

When the FIA finally ended the international career of the 917 the factory were quick to find other uses for the Can-Am. Here Mark Donohue drives the ultimate and most powerful variant the 917/30 of 1973. Through turbocharging the car was made to give up to 1100bhp. The escalating costs of this type of racing coupled with the fact that Porsche had virtually turned it into a one make series panicked the organisers into banning turbocharged cars in the hope that this would provide closer racing and more crowded grids. Unfortunately the opposite proved true with the result that the series had to be abandoned within two years of the ruling.

twenty-five cars of the type in Porsche's front yard took a mere nine months and a reputed 15 million Dm was spent in all on the programme. At the end of the day the brutal machine did what was asked of it and as it improved it kept the World Endurance crown firmly upon the trophy shelf at Zuffenhausen.

By the time the opposition in the shape of Ferrari had developed an answer to the 917 the FIA in its wisdom had closed the loophole in the regulations which had allowed these super beasts to race in the first place, but by then Porsche had scooped the first three of nine World Championships for Makes. In the process they had not only steamrollered the opposition on the race tracks but had caught people's imagination world wide. Even Hollywood had moved in, personified by Steve MacQueen who not only played a Porsche works driver but carried the motif through into his private life by running a 911 and racing a 917 in certain US races, occasionally in the process coming up against fellow super star Paul Newman doing the same thing.

In 1972 when the rules reverted to the three litre limit the life of the car was prolonged yet again by turbocharging it and making a clean sweep two years running in the Can Am series which had hitherto been very much the private property of the Chevrolet MacLaren team. By 1973 when the car became available for Can Am the price had risen to 450,000 Dm. Still the career of the car remains viable for in 1980 the Kremer brothers, long time tuners and racing exponents of a variety of Porsche products, took the basis of the 917 to create the Kremer CK5 and proved the package competitive against the latest factory machinery.

While the 917's were busy making the name of the company, rumours began to permeate through to the press that all was not well within the company itself. The whispers and gossip suggested that there was friction between the so-called Austrian and the German branches of the family. In other words between the sons of Ferry Porsche and the equally talented Piech clan.

For the company which had now found itself at the forefront of world

The 911 can be said to have reached its road going zenith with the introduction of the 930 Turbo in 1974. This car remains the fastest available road going Porsche.

Frankfurt 1973. With the cancellation of Project 266 EA for Volkswagen, Porsche chose to show this vehicle as their idea of a long-life vehicle. It gives some idea of the shape the stillborn 'Beetle' replacement would have taken.

automotive thinking this was hardly a healthy state of affairs. To counter these undercurrents the family withdrew from the company taking the position of equal stockholders and leaving Ferry Porsche to head the board as President while the board responsible for the executive management of the company was drawn from long term Porsche employees under the determined leadership of Dipl Ing Ernst Furhmann who had been the designer of the legendary 547 Spyder engine in the fifties.

This decision became final in 1972 since when the only overt signs of friction in the camp have been the widely quoted comments on company policy made by Ferdinand Piech from his position as head of Audi. Indeed in 1980 it seemed likely that Piech would return to head the company bearing his grandfather's name but instead an American Peter W. Schutz was appointed to the hot seat and Ferdinand Piech lends his considerable talent to keeping the rejuvenated Audi company at the total forefront of world automotive design.

At the time that the company was becoming less of a family concern, more of an international corporation, a rare oddball emerged from the factory in the shape of the new 916. The car was basically a mating of the 914/6 chassis with the newly introduced 2.4 version of the six cylinder 901 engine. Unfortunately it proved too expensive to market although an initial run of eleven cars found enthusiastic owners within the family and those close enough to the company to be offered the new machines. More realistic was the new 911 with this same 2.4 190bhp engine and the resultant changes which were to be made to the car in the light of the fabulous forthcoming 930 Turbo.

The 930 Turbo (known in the UK as the 911 Turbo) made its debut in 1974, a street version it seemed of the 1973 Carrera RSR which had staggered the racing world by taking on the factory prototypes at the Daytona twenty-four hours in 1973 and beaten them fair and square. Admittedly there were those, they still exist, who felt that the Turbo was less in keeping with the proper image of road-going high performance Porsche than the 2.7 litre Carrera of 1973, but nevertheless, the Turbo was the car to place Porsche into that exclusive category of supercars which had previously just eluded them.

From the Turbo sprung the cars which have kept Porsche at the forefront of endurance racing: the 936 Turbo Spyder, the 934 and the all conquering 935 and latterly the ultra high technology 956. To list the achievements of these cars would need a book in its own right, perhaps even to list the engine modifications for each one. But these cars have kept Porsche at the highest pinnacle of the performance and racing world, both in factory teams and private hands and form an integral part of the story of the front engined cars. So too do the three litre and then the three point three litre 911's, for these are the cars which have stayed in the enthusiast's mind and formed his preferences whilst the factory have moved on to newer projects. Projects that they feel are as exciting as the original 356 coupé which emerged from the war-straitened Gmund plant in 1948 and began the age of the rear engined Porsche.

Part Two

The New Generation

Whilst under Fuhrmann the factory had become more efficient and the 911 was still receiving the benefits of a full development programme and profiting from the success of the 934 and 935 series cars; these cars closely resembled the road cars yet managed to humble the specialist prototypes of Porsche's competitors. Each year profits rose and sales increased but so did the difficulties of keeping the beautiful rear engined coupés in line with changing world regulations.

While an engine which runs cleanly can be made to be extremely efficient it does not necessarily become quieter in the process and if the means of measuring the car's overall noise levels are from a certain set position it obviously helps to distance the exhaust noise from the mechanical noise of the engine. Thus, with the United States leading the way as far as restrictive legislation relating to noise, pollution and overall passive vehicle safety Porsche engineers began to evaluate the possible successor to the 911 series in 1968.

The most obvious route to go was seen as an adaptation of the mechanical components of the current design project, EA 266, for a VW Beetle replacement. In essence this would have given the company an extremely sophisticated in-line flat-four liquid cooled engine which it had been planned to lay flat between the rear wheels and under the rear seat of the proposed new VW saloon. This plan came to nothing in 1970, when the newly appointed Rudolf Lieding cancelled the design in preference for what was later to emerge as the 'Golf/Rabbit' range of cars from his own design studios.

Another plan was evolved in 1969 by Helmuth Bott in the design and development works at Weissach. This was uncompromisingly new and relied heavily upon new technology to combat the forest of legislation

1976 and as the 924 struggles to convince the world that it really is a Porsche even though the engine is at the 'other end' and cooled by liquid the factory was busy showing the world its latest racing machinery. The 936 looks the part of the direct descendent of the 917 but the 935's obvious similarity to the 911 can only have strengthened the Porsche traditionalist's view that the rear engine and air cooling was the 'real' Zuffenhausen product.

Original 1976 press release photo for the 924.

53

The 924, seen here in the 'Lux' incarnation. Although development began a year after that of the 928, introduction preceded it by a year.

then being proposed by almost every civilised government. It was this plan which was adopted by Fuhrmann as the long term successor to the 911 and it was finally allowed to proceed with full board backing in 1971 two years after Ferry Porsche had been quoted in the press as saying that the cooling of the engine be it by air or water was immaterial, the real importance of the design was that it worked well. This was almost sacrilege to the current Porsche buff who revelled as much in the uniqueness of the layout and propulsion of his car as he did in the

At its introduction the 928.

amount of attention to technique needed to control it.

This car was the 928 and from the very beginning it was seen as the top car designate in the Porsche range. A rival to the Mercedes Benz 450 SL of the Jaguar and Ferrari top range Grand Touring cars. Noise regulations were allowed to dictate the positioning of the water cooled engine in the front while a high polar moment of inertia was assured by carrying the gear box in conjunction with the differential at the rear. The body was to incorporate all passive design thinking then current whilst being stylish enough to resist the prevailing fashions in car styling and remain current towards the year 2000, thus saving in retooling costs and assuring a continuation of the 911 'constant development' thinking.

Part of the 928 production line at Porsche's Zuffenhausen plant. Here final assembly is taking place.

The proud parent! Ferry Porsche with his Turbo and his 928S in 1980 at the Feurbacher Heide.

The 928S introduced in 1980 seen here in British Series two guise.

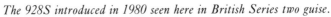

The 924 Carrera complete with deformable plastic wheel arch extensions. The bodywork allowed testing of the 944 to take place on public roads such was the similarity between the two models.

Le Mans 1980 and Andy Rouse brings the car he shared with Tony Dron into twelfth place. For some hours the car had been running on only three cylinders due to an exhaust valve failure. Note the Union Jack motif on the rear wheel arch.

The car which at present carries the full weight of Porsche World Championship challenge, 956.

Announced to the press as the 924 GTR Le Mans and bearing Walter Rohl's name this was the first the world was to see of the 944 engine.

Still as fresh and stylish as ever, the 1984 3.3 litre 930 Turbo is the fastest and most expensive of all the road cars

Just previous to the board's adoption, however, a replacement for the VW-Porsche 914 was commissioned by VAG. Codenamed EA 425, this was to become the 924, the car was to use the Audi 2 litre four cylinder engine and to draw the majority of its components from the VW parts racks. The radical thinking behind the 928 was to find its way into the car at all levels, in the layout of the major components, the body styling and the need to meet international legislative requirements for many years to come. Like the 928 it was also to be demonstrably fuel efficient.

This project was cancelled by the next VW chief, Toni Schmucker after the first really bad petrol crisis in 1973. This time, however, the car was saved by the timely intervention of Porsche's marketing staff who had begun to realise that a hole existed in the bottom end of the market which the traditional names within the industry were not in any position, due to conservatism or over estimation of the effects of the newer restrictive legislation in the US market, to supply.

It has been said, probably with some justification, that had the 924 arrived in the market place as an Audi the reception would have been totally overwhelming with only the good points singled out for attention. It did not, however, and to a certain extent probably drew as much flack from the general public who thought any new Porsche should be both faster and more radical than those already on sale, as it did from the traditional Porsche enthusiast who saw only a sell out of the rear air cooled engine layout.

Admittedly the 924 as first introduced certainly fell far short of most enthusiasts' ideal Zuffenhausen product. The engine was shared both with the current Audi 100 and the VW LT31 van. It was fitted with K Jetronic fuel injection and in European trim developed some 125bhp at 5,800rpm. The claimed top speed was 124mph and a 0-60mph time of ten seconds was well within the capabilities of most road testers. Seen as a rival to the outmoded MGB GT or the thirsty but faster Datsun 260Z it was fine but it left many journalists puzzled as to the reasons behind the decision to market the car in the first place.

Coming as it did at the end of 1976 in time for the 1977 model year the car found itself the butt of a lot of not wholly unjustified criticism. The price was felt to be too high, although the base price was soon rendered obsolete by the next round of oil induced price rises throughout the world's car markets. The fairly spartan interior received its fair share of abuse as well, although the front seats with their 911 heritage found universal favour.

The VW-based suspension was praised although several journalists felt that the pressed steel wheels with 165×14 tyres were somewhat basic. 185×14 tyres on six inch alloy wheels were listed from the beginning as optional equipment as were gas filled Bilsteins and leather upholstery. The body was protected by hot dipping.

As with the 928, Porsche had opted for the transaxle layout with the clutch at the front and the two metre long drive shaft supported by four bearings within the carrying tube, which is itself mounted in rubber to cut down on transmitted noise and vibration. The greater loads put on the cogs by this type of transmission were provided for by making the synchro rings of molybdenum. The final drive was some 3.44:1 as opposed to the original 3.77:1.

Steering was rack and pinion with four turns lock to lock, brakes were disc front and drums rear, the drums coming, like the Macpherson strut front and semi-trailing link rear suspension from the VW 1303, with servo and dual circuit split diagonally. From the 914 came the main dials, switches and various other interior fitments from the VW Golf whilst the door handles came from the Beetle.

The positioning of the gear box allowed a 48 percent front 52 percent rear weight distribution which made for extremely fine control on most surfaces; these facets of the car being the true heritage of the Porsche design department. The yaw factor was also extremely low whilst the quoted Cd factor of .36 was more than acceptable in those days.

The 914 had always been a far better seller in the USA than any of the company's other territories and it was to the credit of the engineers at Porsche that they managed to keep the power loss down to just 10bhp on the federalised version. It was with the USA primarily in mind that the option list also included such items as air conditioning sun roof, headlamp wipe and wash and tinted glass. In all the launch of the 924 was handled as far as possible to retain the loyalty of those who were perhaps looking to replace their mid engined 914 with a more convenient 2+2 with lower maintenance costs and (at least in the case of the 914/4) superior performance.

It was with the US market firmly in mind that Porsche chose the 924 to launch its first ever fully automatic car. The box chosen was the Audi three speed which was again mounted in the rear 'transaxle' position. Again the power loss was kept to a minimum. The fuel consumption increased overall by some eight percent while some eight miles per hour were lost from the maximum speed. Concurrently a five speed box was introduced which added an overdrive top and allowed the third and fourth gear ratios to be brought closer giving a smoother power spread. This box was to prove unpopular in certain market territories because of the positioning of reverse gear being below first as in most lightweight racing boxes eventually leading the factory to adopt the Audi five speed box, installation being facilitated by changing the position of the box from the front to the back of the differential.

At the time of the 924 introduction the Porsche management fielded questions about the adoption of the transaxle system over the standard front wheel drive system both by explaining the weight distribution factors involved and by saying that the transaxle could be adapted to transmit more power far more efficiently than front wheel drive. Whilst the car was giving only 125bhp in European trim or 115bhp Federalised this seemed a fairly negative line of reasoning. In the press, however, speculation that a new more powerful engine was eventually planned lasted for several months fuelled also by reports from various German journalists that a new turbocharged engine was definitely on the cards.

That the car needed a more sporting image was recognised within the factory and by 1978 several cars were beginning to be seen on the racing circuits of the world with the British importer leading the way with a fairly up-market one-make challenge series won easily by Tony Dron. Later the British also took the Commander's Cup, an almost forgotten trophy for a twenty-four hour endurance test at the Snetterton circuit, carefully timed to provide the best possible trade press coverage.

In the States the cars were used as pace cars where their more powerful stablemates were in definite contention for overall honours. Special editions were offered in lookalike form whilst a worldwide marketing exercise was launched with a Martini liveried special edition when the team cars took the World Championship for Makes. Cars prepared by various privateers and Porsche dealers started to compete successfully in Group D racing in the States with the factory supplying special lightweight equipment. All this was fine but it still had very few spin-offs to the average owner. In 1979 all this was righted by the appearance of the 924 Turbo.

The 924 Turbo was destined, for a few years at least, to become all things to all Porsche lovers. At last the performance was acceptable to the traditional customer, the styling had become more familiar since the launch and as a basis for real competition it slotted nicely into the picture which the family had carefully nurtured over the years of the company being totally committed to racing as both an aid to development and to marketing.

Admittedly the price was high but the factory could with impunity point out that nowhere else could the prospective customer buy the kind of performance the car offered for anything near the money. They could also point out that when driven at the same speeds the car would return better consumption than its normally aspirated parent. In short they had produced a car which could finally silence the 'knockers'.

The factory claimed a maximum speed for the car as announced of some 140mph. Later several testers found this to be conservative. This, however, was still fast enough to put the car firmly at the forefront of the company's own product performance league. Only the 930 Turbo, the 928 and 928S were actually faster and in each case the price amply held these products from the market which would once have made the 356 its premier choice in the car market.

The package offered for the Turbo was restrained to say the least. Aerodynamically it was felt necessary to add a chin spoiler and the rear airflow was cleaned up a little with a moulding below the rear hatch which soon became de rigueur for all 924's. Openings were cut in the nose for air ducts to feed the oil cooler and brakes and a 'NACA' duct carried air flow to the engine. A new two branch exhaust of larger diameter than the normally aspirated vehicle put back some of the sporting sound which the turbocharger damped out and a two tone optional paint job with attractive new alloy wheels helped boost the cosmetics slightly.

Mechanically the obvious changes to handle the 170bhp which the car gave in European trim were mainly in the suspension and braking area. The front suspension was beefed up to compensate for the additional weight of the turbo installation and a stronger rear anti roll bar was incorporated. The steering was lightened by some 5 percent by the adoption of a different rack. The car was fitted with ventilated disc brakes all round and a new nine inch servo helped to enforce their effectiveness. The parking brake was moved inboard to its exclusive drum location much as on the 928. At first however, these brakes were not deemed necessary for the Federalised cars which were restricted to 150bhp, and US spec cars were still delivered with the standard car's disc and drum set up. This was soon changed under pressure from US dealers who felt somewhat slighted by the Germans on this score.

With the engine the Porsche engineers had evolved a superb package based around the KKK turbocharger and using a waste gate to cut down on the throttle lag which had dogged all road car applications of exhaust driven forced induction until that time. Even they however could not disguise the slight lag which must always attend such installations as numerous testers and owners were to find when encountering the cut-in of boost on a damp or badly cambered bend. None the less both press and owners felt that at last some positive effort had been made in this direction.

The lack of available space under the bonnet of the standard car plus the bulk of the installation caused the engineers to deliberate long and hard on the positioning of the unit. Eventually it was decided to place the turbo close up to the manifold above the steering rack, move the starter motor to the opposite side of the engine, position the by pass valve well below the exhaust manifold, leaving room for the US catalytic converter and bring the pressurised air across the top of the engine to feed the K Jetronic injection.

The cylinder head and pistons were redesigned to give a cleaner, almost spherical combusiton area and much attention was given to the gasketting to allay the effects of the extra heat created by the new set up. The inlet valves were increased in size from 36mm to 40mm whilst the exhaust valves grew from 33 to 36mm. The spark plugs were repositioned towards the inlet side of the head, again in search of further thermal efficiency, to this end platinum pointed plugs were employed.

To cope with the extra torque, some 180lb/ft (24.5mkg) the drive shaft was increased in thickness by 5mm. Easier servicing was ensured by the use of transistorised electronic ignition and this also helped to keep throttle surge to a minimum. Further protection against this was facilitated by the use of a pressure relief valve on the compressor housing. As introduced the turbo was safe to some 90,000rpm and gave up to 10lb psi boost. The compression ratio of the European model was 7.5:1 giving a nominal figure with boost of 10.8:1. For the US model this gave an official figure of 143bhp at 5500rpm with torque rated at 147lb/ft.

Now, by incorporating some of the lightweight parts developed for the SCCA group D racers the factory had a real basis for an assault on the race tracks of Europe. Sure enough the 'Carrera' version wasn't long in coming.

Just as in the fifties when the first Carrera arrived the 924 Carrera became an instant success. Admittedly there was something less than finished about its newly acquired body tuning parts, the flared arches seemingly having been borrowed from some similar but not altogether identical vehicle, the spoilers having a sort of brutal half-conceived look and the colour keying making the whole look somewhat unfinished to eyes more accustomed to 'Porsche Perfection'. These minor details seemed rather to complement the purposeful look of the beast than detract from it.

The roadtesters in the specialist press had finally found the front-engined Porsche they so desired. Within months the limited edition was sold out worldwide and now a good example can fetch almost its showroom cost when offered on the used car market. It was the car the enthusiast had been waiting for, but most important it presaged the debut of the 924 Turbo at the classic Le Mans twenty-four hour race in June 1980.

Giving 210bhp at 6000rpm the customer Carrera GT was very near to the cars which finally took the grid at the Sarthe circuit. Weight was saved by using thinner steel in the general bodywork, alloy bonnet and doors. GFR plastic was used in the spoilers and arch flares and ultra light Porsche alloy wheels completed the package which lightened the basic production Turbo by some 180kg.

Other race related hardwear incorporated, included stiffer springs with adjustable shocks, a choice of fifteen or sixteen inch diameter wheels a reworked cylinder head, a new crankshaft and new Marelli digital ignition. Inside the driver had the benefit of completely new light-weight seats and the four-spoke leather covered sports steering wheel.

On the Continent these cars were offered as lightweight almost ready to race vehicles with fairly basic specifications. The British importer, however, decided to revive flagging interest in the 924 by using this homologation exercise to launch a special luxury edition of seventy-five vehicles at that year's Birmingham Motor Show. These cars featured such equipment as headlight wiper and wash, electric windows, rear wiper, heated exterior mirror and other such items usually found only on the optional extra list.

The cars for the race at Le Mans were prepared in the glare of the public eye. Extensive testing in February at the Circuit Paul Ricard evaluated such necessary artifacts as tyres, differentials, the new all aluminium drive shaft tube and rear bodywork and all the various sport parts deemed desirable. The company's plan was to run three cars each crewed by drivers from an important Porsche marketing territory. One was to represent the fatherland with a German crew, one would be crewed by Americans and the third by Englishmen in deference to that country having just supplanted Italy as Porsche's largest European market.

The US team never really happened, for a road accident before the race left Englishman Derek Bell sharing a car with American Al Holbert. The German team also mixed two nationalities for whilst Jurgen Barth was German his co-driver Manfred Schurti was from Luxembourg. Only the British team remained racially pure with Tony Dron who had already proved himself the most consistently quick 924 driver in Britain and Andy Rouse who had just put a disastrous season racing the ill-fated Jaguar XJC behind him.

Speaking of the race, Rouse, an extremely highly rated test and development driver commented that, 'It seemed that as drivers we were just a necessary item of equipment on the car. In fact apart from the few laps the factory allowed us at Ricard we never really saw the cars again until Le Mans.' Such are the idiosyncrasies of a successful works team. Indeed conditions for the drivers at Le Mans itself favoured very much the same attitude, for both Dron and Rouse recall the little spartan accommodation available to them which was devoid of shower facilities and electric light until the resourceful Dron managed to procure a light bulb 'from somewhere'.

To say that the cars were a success at the Sarthe circuit would be an understatement. At one time the British car was lying a consistent fourth with the American car closely formated. In fact whilst it rained the cars stood a very real chance for their 49/51 percent weight distribution gave them a vast edge in the handling stakes, abetted by the much narrower tyres which maintained a superior grip on the damp track.

Early morning changed the picture drastically though, for the exhaust valves on the American car began to burn out leaving the car on three cylinders, a state of affairs which was soon duplicated in the British car. Meanwhile the German car lost two laps in the pits after destroying the radiator when a hare ran out onto the thrack. Even so the cars struggled home with the German car a resounding sixth overall and the British and American cars 12th and 13th respectively. As a proving exercise the affair was a triumph of the first order.

Hardly had the plaudits from the race died away when the factory laid down yet another homologation run. This was even more powerful and bore the name Carrera GTS. This time the engine developed a useful 245bhp at 6,250rpm from 14psi boost giving 247ft/lb (34mkg) torque at 3,000rpm. The car sold for some 110,000 Dm. An even more meaty version was built at the same time for competition work. This was the 924 Carrera GTR costing a mere 145,000 Dm. In return it gave up to 375bhp at 6,400rpm coupled with an impressive 298lb/ft (41mkg) torque at 5,600rpm. Meanwhile as the 924 gradually grew more sophisticated and became the largest selling Porsche of all time the 928 had finally reached the public to some very mixed press and customer reactions.

Fuhrmann had originally given the go ahead on the car on October 21st 1971 and by the end of that year plans were already advanced enough for the overall mechanical outline of the car to be decided. Early in 1972 the transaxle set-up for the car was under evaluation in a Mercedes Benz 350SL, codenamed V1 by the works.

By August 1973 full rig tests were carried out on the engine and chassis whilst the suspension was under constant development in a modified Opel Admiral codenamed V2. V3 was the body of an Audi 100 coupé grafted onto the floorpan and engine set up very similar to that which would finally appear as the 928. This was completed on September 19th 1973.

In late January 1974 the decision was taken to use weight saving aluminium and plastics where possible in order to meet the stringent parameters which both Fuhrmann and Ferry Porsche had set for it. The first prototype to be fitted with the first of the weight saving parts, 928 W2 took to the roads in June 1974. By this time the design team had evaluated and rejected double wishbone rear suspension as being too costly in terms of interior space and finalised the rear around a torsion bar set-up. This necessitated a new approach to setting up the car to cure the incipient tuck-in caused by the rear transaxle location. Eventually the factory overcame this problem by adjusting the toe-in of the rear wheels thus prolonging the useful life of one of the founder's most important patents.

50,000 mile tests were undertaken with all the prototypes, the proving grounds varying from Porsche's own test track at Weissach to Algeria to the Arctic circle. The V cars proved themselves useful right up to the beginning of 1977 with more and more parts destined for the finalised production models finding their way in each year. Among the last major components to be finalised were the body pressings themselves, for in the course of development there had been controversy over almost every aspect of the new cars, including at one stage an internal feud as to whether the car should be produced as a two or four door or even whether the car should be produced at all in view of the political situation caused by the ever increasing oil prices.

The first press assessments of the car were cautious in the extreme. Nobody seemed ready to commit themselves in print to any definite stance on the car. Many noted that in its initial form the car was slower than the original E Type Jaguar. Where they wanted to know had the intervening fifteen years' expertise been wasted?

All the press took the view that the essence of a Porsche was in the way that the factory constantly refined and updated the car and seized on this as justification of cataloguing its negative points. Some indeed were justifiably out of place on a car costing as much as the top of the range Mercedes coupé. The lack of space in the rear was popularly condemned as was the unthinking attitude of anyone who could design a car so obviously aimed into the upper end of the US market with so much all up glass area.

As well as criticising the area of the glass most also managed to find some fault with the distribution claiming poor three-quarter vision for such a 'practical exotic'. Very few found much to complain of in the ride and handling characteristics of the cars although the only positive point which found universal acclaim was the superb quietness of the car even under harsh acceleration or unfavourable road surface conditions.

All in all the reaction to the car was decidedly unfavourable and as such it brought forth a welter of defensive statements from the works, statements which were used by the press as proof that the 928 was indeed a 911 replacement regardless of the attitude of the announcements from the board at Porsche which protested that it was a 'new form of car to meet new conditions'.

The world reaction to the car also caused Ferdinand Piech to give vent to bitter invective towards the incumbent management from his position as chief of Audi. His remarks to the effect that the car was not sophisticated enough to be in the tradition of his grandfather and that many practical considerations had been sacrificed to allow a fairly pleasing shape certainly hit the target and the press and the industry used them as further proof that the car fell far short of the type of vehicle needed to head up the list of successors to the illustrious 911.

Being the first sports car to take the once coveted 'Car Of The Year' title should have helped redress some of the more savagely hurt feelings at Zuffenhausen. Instead the title itself became more questioned by the few motoring writers who the public could look to for any independent opinions on what really went on in the industry. Admittedly the initial press reactions, leaving aside the high drag coefficient, and high fuel consumption were tempered by quite a degree of acceptance for its looks. But at the end of the day Porsche realised that they had underestimated the needs of those who wanted a new Porsche and did not fall into the category of the middle-aged autobahn-cruising self-employed German businessman at whom the car was blatantly aimed. A solution had to be found.

It was common knowledge that Fuhrmann had something special up his sleeve with regard to the 928. Porsche watchers noted the fact that he himself used a special turbocharged version of the car. They quoted the technical staff as saying that the development potential for the engine had yet to be exploited and lastly they pointed out that never had the factory led with its most powerful model.

Intriguingly the Porsche staff kept speculation about the ultimate 928 bubbling with teasing little leaks. The 928S when it arrived in 1980 must have been the worst kept secret in the German automotive industry. Its immediate effect was stunning. There can be little doubt that would-be Porsche owners, the press and those already in possession of the rear engined cars wanted to welcome this new generation car from the off. The 928S gave them a chance to re-accept and re-evaluate and as such the car was no longer found wanting.

True, Porsche had upgraded the performance and smoothed out some of the more niggling aspects of the car yet, as more than one customer was to point out, what real difference could there be between a car which travels at one hundred and fifty and does it in style and one which travels some five miles per hour faster and achieves it with little noticeable difference.

The basis of the car was still exactly the same. The same technology was used, true certain engine modifications had been incorporated; the bore had increased from 95 to 97mm to increase the capacity to 4,664cc; compression had been increased on both versions of the car to 10:1 (from 8.5:1 as introduced on the basic 928); different cams had been incorporated to complement the straight through exhausts and the breathing had been 'improved' by the use of larger valves. Some 60 brake horse power was thus added to the S and the maximum torque had been improved slightly from 280lb/ft at 3,600rpm, to 284lb/ft at 4,500rpm encouraging the driver to make much better use of the available revs.

From the outside the main difference between the 928 and the 928S are minor ones such as the front spoiler and rear air dam and the less sculpted alloy wheels. The same driver comfort that so characterises the 928 was transferred without change except for the standardisation of certain upholstery finishes and the addition of some newer optional fabrics. A selection of metallic finishes which the factory also offered as options on the basic 928 also became standard on the 'S'.

A factor which had been heavily criticised at the launch of the 928 was its high Cd factor in respect of its low profile, some press sources quoting as high as .42, the addition of new tyres, wheels and the spoilers allowed the 'S' to drop to a more respectable 0.38. Fuel consumption which had been a major issue with the 928 was also an area that had been slightly rectified. By raising the compression both cars were returning in the region of 16mpg, which by any standards is hardly bad for cars with such capabilities.

At the launch in 1964 of the 911 much had been made of the Biral method of casting the cylinder blocks. This was a process which allowed the bonding of the sophisticated aluminium castings needed to cool the engine with the cast iron liners needed to ensure long engine life. Likewise with the launch of the 928 one of the outstanding features as far as the technical press were concerned was the use of the Reynolds method of casting the V8 block.

This method using a high silicon aluminium alloy, usually extremely brittle, allows the pistons to run directly in the bores without liners. In effect a layer of silicon crystals stands some one thousandth of a milimetre proud of the surrounding alloy and formed a basis for oil to form about them. It was a process perfected in the huge eight litre Can Am engines, used by the mighty General Motors combine in the Chevrolet Vega engine and now used for the first time within the intricate casting patterns of what must almost be a 'mass' production all alloy V8.

Another area of constant irritation in the early 928 was the over sophisticated electronic warning system which seemed to have a built-in propensity for showing the most dire warnings at the drop of any unrelated switch. This situation was a little rectified with the 1980 cars but still occasionally gave misleading information as two or three leading road testers pointed out.

Perhaps because the 928S gave a more 'Porsche Like' performance a number of the sporting press took the opportunity of its launch to point out that the project leader on the 928, Helmut Flegl (currently Director of Research) was responsible for chassis design on the 917. Although judging by the remarks of the drivers who first encountered the 917 this might have been a two edged sword, but it showed once again how much the press wanted to be seen to accommodate this car which they still found difficult placing into any relevant market 'slot'.

By now the lines of the car began to be accepted for what they were, an extremely sleek and functionally beautiful package amply provided to meet legislative changes into the twenty first century. The use of composite materials in the crushable zones had also been open to question at the launch of the car. After almost three years it could be seen that these were not only functional but that they remained perfectly colour durable and free from distortion even after the occasional minor shunt.

On the sales front the car had exceeded all original targets set for it, although in fairness it should be pointed out that as with the launch of the 911 various informed people within the compass of the factory were saying that these had been kept low. With the advent of the 'S' the car was set to conquer yet further markets, for until this point the car had not seriously demonstrated any ability to take customers from the likes of Ferrari, Lamborghini or such cars as the BMW M1. Admittedly the factory showed no inclination to race the 928 but with the supreme success of the current 935 and the waxing reputation of the 924 GTR they could easily argue that there was no real need to do so.

This then was the state of play as Le Mans 1981 drew near and speculation began to become rife that yet another 'new generation' car could be expected from Zuffenhausen.

Part Three

The 944

Le Mans 1981 was a race of mixed fortunes for all concerned. For the factory it was a complete triumph with Ickx taking his fifth outright victory paired with Derek Bell in a Jules-sponsored 936. The locally based Rondeau team took second and third once the second works 936 had lost an hour with gearbox troubles, although their achievement was marred by the death in a high speed crash of Jean-Louis Lafosse. For Ferrari fans the fifth placing of what was basically a slightly modified 512 BB gave some hope of renewed factory involvement and for the marketing department at Zuffenhausen it was a red letter day as European Rally Champion Walter Rohl together with Sigi Brun and Jurgen Barth brought a 924 Carrera with a very special engine into a highly commendable seventh place.

For Rohl it was a first experience of Le Mans and to date he has declined to further it, although for a while earlier in that year he had been seen in a privately entered, but works supported, 924 GTS on selected European Rallies. The car that he and his co-drivers had been putting through its paces was what was subsequently to be known as the second generation of front engined cars, the 944.

As a first appearance the car put up an impressive showing, for although its KKK turbocharged oversquare engine with its four valve twin cam head delivered a highly respectable 410bhp at 6500rpm it was certainly not in the league of the various other top line prototype machinery present. Proudly Porsche pointed out that the car had run to strict team orders and that in the process of doing so it had spent less time in the pits than any other car in the race. An auspicious debut to say the least.

Within days of the race Porsche Public Relations staff world wide were issuing a new press release. In Great Britain Michael Cotton headed his '944: A NEW PORSCHE!' and began; 'The Porsche range will be extended next year when the new 944 goes into production. The 944, which has an entirely new Porsche 2.5 litre engine bristling with advanced features, will make its debut at the Frankfurt Show in September and will go into production at the end of the year...'

The release went on to tell how the 944 would resemble the 924 Carrera but be fabricated entirely in galvanised steel and be covered by Porsche's seven year anti rust guarantee before beginning to detail the engine and major mechanical components. Throughout the release the tone was one of uncontrived technical triumph. Porsche knew from the beginning that what they had was good and the release was letting the press into it.

The body shape of the 944 was probably the first of any Porsche to owe more detail refinement to the wind tunnel than to the design team's ideals. Having taken a lot of largely ill informed criticism on the relatively high drag coefficient of the 928 the men at Zuffenhausen were

The Ickx/Bell 936 leading Le Mans in 1981 with the Barth/Brun/Rohl 944 in the background.

Originally entered as the 924 GTS Le Mans the 944 as seen on the track in June 1981 was due to spend less time in the pits than any other car in the race on its way to a magnificent overall seventh place. As can be seen, apart from the air scoop and the extra track width necessitating wider rear wheel arches the car looked remarkably like the standard 944.

Frontal view shows the increased track width necessary for racing.

certainly making sure with this one that the same would not be said of their latest offering. The official Porsche literature made this clear from the outset by treating the aerodynamics as a subject in its own right in the very front of the brochure.

'Reducing the much talked about drag coefficient alone does not achieve the desired objective of lower fuel consumption and/or higher performance,' the lectured. 'In terms of wind resistance, the frontal area is at least as important as the Cw (drag) factor.' (Cd factor in UK.) As soon as the first testers managed to put the car on the road it was obvious that the time Porsche had spent on the aerodynamics had paid good dividends.

The handling of any car at high speed must to some extent be dependent on such factors as the position of the aerodynamic pressure point and its relation to the amount of lift generated by the air flow beneath the front of the car. In the 944 much effort had been put into optimising these two factors and cutting down on underbody turbulence. Thought was expended also on the rear cut-off point for the air in a quest to optimise the pressure on the driving wheels at speed, thus in conjunction with the transaxle layout minimising risks from cross winds and traffic turbulence at high speed.

The research which had gone into making the 924 Carrera more suited to the world's race tracks also paid dividends in such areas as water dissipation, wind noise and engine ventilation. The ride which most testers had criticised in the 924 was praised by most in the new car but almost all complained of a higher level of road noise although some admitted that the overall quietness of the car did tend to highlight this.

To those familiar with the way Porsche tend to evolve models rather than create them the blending of the 924 with certain facets of the 928 came as no surprise. Thus the fact that the engine was roughly equivalent to one half of the 928 engine actually surprised no-one. Like its bigger parent it too used the Reynolds alloy and needed no linings. Like its predecessor it also used iron sprayed piston with sintered GKN connecting rods.

Perhaps the most advantageous angle from which to display the 944 is this upper front threequarter shot from the press department at Zuffenhausen. Even standing still the smoothly sculpted and curvacious lines give a distinct impression of speed, heightened by the gently banked surface of the track.

Seen head-on the wide track, small frontal area and extremely tidy wheel arch moulding is highlighted.

From the same pre release photo session the car seen at speed from the lower three quarter angle.

That the engine had been increased in size from what would naturally constitute half of the 928S unit by oversquaring the bore to exactly 100mm gave Porsche enthusiasts some idea that the five litre V8 might some day become a reality. On the launch of the car, however, the engine designer Gerhard Kirchendorffer was quoted by Rex Greenslade writing in *Motor* as saying that the engine in four cylinder form could very easily be taken to 2.7 litres thus opening the very interesting proposition that one day the world could see a 5.4 litre 928S.

In deciding to enlarge the bore and leave the stroke at 78.9mm the design team at Porsche were making allowance for the bottom end of the engine to be built on the same machinery as the 928, thus maximising the cross over of components as far as possible. A spin off however is that with such oversquare engines usually an extremely good performance/economy ratio can be achieved by using high compression ratios. With their TOP system Porsche were able to exploit this to give extremely good economy without sacrifice in terms of either torque or brake horsepower.

As if to draw attention to the fact that the car was refined as well as fast the publicity department took pains to set the car in this tranquil environment. From the side the car is less photogenic the resemblance to the 924 being heavily highlighted by the silhouette and window lines.

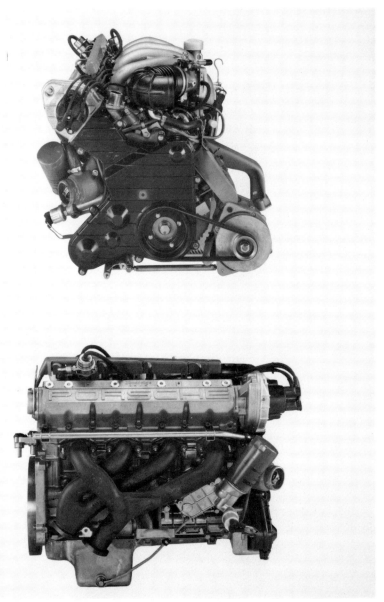

Front and side elevations of the engine. Note the extremely clean lines of both inlet and exhaust manifolds which represent an extremely sophisticated casting process. As can be seen the belts which drive the overhead camshaft and balance shafts can be reached easily by detaching a cover, thus simplifying replacement or routine inspection.

This cutaway gives a good view of the hydraulic tappets and electronic control system.

Here the intricate external castings are displayed to fine effect.

Here the clean lines of the outlet manifold can be seen to advantage.

In effect the TOP system (the letters stand for Thermodynamically Optimized Porsche) allows an extremely high compression rate while avoiding pre-detonation by means of using a supremely efficient turbulence pattern in the combustion chamber. This chamber in the 944 engine is of an inclined wedge shape the edges of which are overlapped by the piston. The narrow edge of the wedge is opposite the spark plug, thus as the compression takes place the majority of the mixture swirls towards the higher end of this wedge shape and so towards the spark. Simple in essence, extremely complicated in practice this method allows high levels of economy at cruising speeds whilst still providing the efficiency needed to provide the kind of acceleration that buyers expect in high performance cars.

To feed this new and efficient engine Porsche abandoned their long term affiliation to K Jetronic injection to substitute the less sophisticated L Jetronic. However the electronic control which had become possible with the mass adaptation of microelectronics allowed firing to be so rigorously accurate that the more complicated system was deemed unnecessary in this application.

With an engine depending heavily on the expansion rate between the cylinder walls and the pistons staying constant, lubrication has to be a vital consideration. Porsche chose to take care of this problem by mounting a sickle type pump on the front of the crankshaft feeding through a maze of meticulously cast oil channels. To maintain a constantly viable temperature, however, Porsche incorporated an inter-cooler whereby the coolant of the engine speeds the warm-up period of the oil and once warmed helps to maintain the correct ambient temperature. Because of the complicated casting structure a very sophisticated oil scavenge system with a minimum of air access was deemed necessary and Porsche provided this within the structure of the oil galleries themselves.

The advantages of a large torquey four cylinder motor for performance cars have been recognised for years, but until the advent of the 944 the maximum deemed advisable regarding cubic capacity was the 2.3 litre ohc General Motors unit used most recently in the larger four cylinder Vauxhall cars. The simple reason for this lies in the secondary vibrations set up by the wide timing intervals and the implausibility of four non-reciprocating masses operating in the same plane. At low engine speeds these vibrations cause few problems if the engine mountings are tuned properly and the masses being moved are not unduly large. In many engines it is possible to design out the vibrations in the normal rev range but this does not actually cure the problem. With the larger engine these solutions do not apply, the only successful alleviation was that designed by Dr. Frederick Lanchester and patented by him under the numbers 26,038 and 26,777 in 1911 for two counter-rotating out-of-balance shafts turning at twice crankshaft speed and driven by chain or helical (worm) gearing. This became known as the Lanchester Harmonic Balancer and resurfaced in the late seventies with a further modification by those clever fellows at Mitsubishi which enabled the two shafts to be mounted at different levels and driven by toothed belts.

By sacrificing the four brake horse power needed to drive them and incorporating these shafts Porsche found a way to make the engine free revving. The final smoothness however, came from novel engine mounts which function on the transference of glycol from one interior chamber

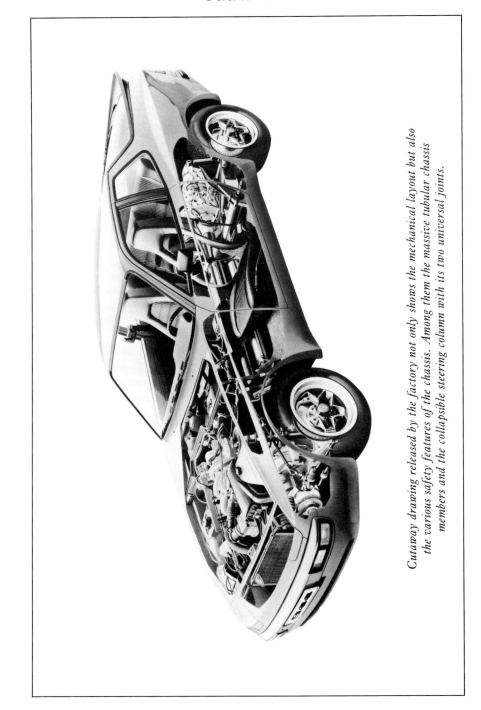

Cutaway drawing released by the factory not only shows the mechanical layout but also the various safety features of the chassis. Among them the massive tubular chassis members and the collapsible steering column with its two universal joints.

Not content with merely providing a cutaway drawing the factory went one better and provided this cutaway car. Porsche take pains to point out, however, that this is no mere exhibition crowd puller but a serious aid to training both factory staff and mechanics.

The vehicle illustrates the amount of thought and effort which has gone into obtaining the highest possible utilisation of the available interior space both in the passenger and in the engine compartments.

to another to prevent the remaining vibrations from transmitting to the chassis.

The valves and valve gear are also a potential source of vibration in an engine. As in the 928 the 944 carries its valves mounted almost vertically in the heads, operated by a single overhead camshaft. This vibration is overcome by means of damping and lifting pulleys, the drive belts are mounted outside the block for ease of maintenance and also drive the balance shafts. Again, as on the 928, hydraulic tappets are employed to reduce maintenance.

As introduced this engine provided some 163bhp at 5,800rpm with an electric cut out limiting engine speeds to 6500rpm. With the available power and the smoothness of the unit this has proved an extremely worthwhile addition to the other standard features. More than one road tester and the author have found the device cutting-in in the intermediate gears, thereby saving what could eventually be an expensive engine rebuild or worse. Torque is rated at some 151lb/ft at 3,000rpm thus giving the driver the benefit of extreme flexibility although relatively high gear ratios are utilised.

The TOP engine with its digital ignition system allows the engine to run at a normal compression ratio of 10.6:1. However when cruising on part throttle the mixture can be leaned as far as 17:1 with no adverse effect. When this is taken into account with the high torque and the higher gearing that this facilitates, extremely good economy was achieved in all normal driving conditions. Thus when introduced the official figures for consumption were 40.4mpg at 56mph, 32.5 at 75mph with the urban cycle giving a frugal 24.8mpg. In the US these figures equate to 33.7mpg at 56mph, 27.1mpg at 75mph with the urban cycle set at 20.7. Figures almost unknown in previous high performance cars and

To make certain that all advantages can be derived the cutaway car also features the cut away engine.

figures which proved remarkably accurate in the light of subsequent road tests.

Going back to the advent of the 924 and the VW project 425 which brought about its evolution it will be remembered that the brief which the designers in Zuffenhausen were working to was a very different type than they would have been involved with had the project been for a smaller Porsche from the word go. The number of proprietary VW parts would have been to a higher standard (although of course Porsche did incorporate the seats from the 911) and the design would probably have differed in the knowledge that whilst a massive combine like VAG can afford to retool to meet changing fashions in bodystyling on a fairly frequent basis, a smaller specialist producer like Porsche would be crippled by this amount of capital reallocation.

It made sense therefore in a number of ways that when Porsche bought back the 924 design they opted to fall in line with a VW overture to produce the car in the old NSU plant at Neckarsulm. The main benefits to Porsche were immediately obvious; for Neckarsulm is just

In profile the cut away car amply demonstrates the box sections which constitute an integral drivers safety cage. Also the strong tubular seat sub frames and carefully contoured padding.

forty minutes away from Zuffenhausen by Autobahn, and close to Heilbron, thus assuring a highly skilled workforce. The Neckarsulm plant has regularly topped the VAG table of plants for quality control procedure and had ample capacity if the 924 became a runaway success to meet that demand.

From the other side it allowed VAG to keep the old NSU plant open in the face of union pressure when in time they would have probably been forced into closing it for economic reasons. There was also the logistical advantage of centralising parts delivery, buying procedures and all the rest of the advantages extra capacity can bring. In fact so successful was the cooperation that the VAG group are now modernising the plant to keep it in service well into the twenty-first century and beyond.

Admittedly certain quality control problems arose at the beginning of the two companies cooperation but certainly such defects which did manifest in the early 924 were soon overcome. In fact to any interested observer the quality of finish from Neckarsulm on both the cars that they build for Porsche and on Audi's own 80 reflect probably the highest of any plant in Europe for mass production. By 1981 when the one hundred thousandth 924 left the plant, thus establishing the model as Porsche's largest selling ever, much detail modification both to the car and the manufacturing processes had taken place.

In the case of the 924 Carrera the whole engine assembly was put together in Zuffenhausen whilst the design of the four cylinder engine had been constantly updated until L. J. K. Setright writing in *Car* in September 1982 could justifiably remark that very little of the original design remained current. The hot dip cataphoretic process with which the cars were protected against rust had been so far improved that Porsche confidently extended their anti-corrosion guarantee for a further year from six to seven years and the warranty claim rate was the lowest of any in the VAG empire.

Having said this it must however be pointed out that the lifespan of the four cylinder two litre engine was known from the start to be limited. Its death knell was well and truly sounded by the advent of the unique Audi five which just would not fit the 924. Thus although VW offered to produce the two litre engine for as long as Porsche might care to use it, logically the introduction of the 944 unit was extremely timely. The fact that it could be assembled by the workforce at Zuffenhausen and then taken with a minimum of inconvenience to Neckarsulm also augered well for the pricing of this car and for the continuing expansion of the work force at Porsche.

Unlike the engine the gear box which Audi now provided both for the 924 and the 944 showed no sign of approaching obsolescence. The five speed which was incorporated in the 944 had first been adopted for the 924 in 1980 thus giving the 924 owner the same change pattern as that of the 911SC and most other rational five speed vehicles. In order to mate the box to the new engine all that was necessary was a change in ratios thus easing the production engineer's task and helping to keep the price of the new car within reach of the targetted market.

Also in common with the 924 the VW three speed automatic box was offered as an optional fitting. When deciding to do this Porsche must definitely have had the company executive firmly in mind, for originally this feature had been adopted for the US market yet proved to be a boon for the corporate customer to whom the image and prestige of the name Porsche could easily take second place to the thought of constant gear shifting whilst using the car heavily in urban driving.

This overhead view shows to fine effect the airflow patterns obtained by intensive wind tunnel development. This smoothness in the airflow not only allows greater economy and performance but also gives a quieter high speed ride to lack of wind buffeting.

With both transmission alternatives a limited slip differential is offered. Set at 40% it takes the form of two friction plates located in the differential housing activated by the torque input from the drive shafts. For those unfamiliar with the function of this device it acts as a limiter on the power supplied to either wheel in the case of one losing traction. This tends to increase the driveability of the car and especially to enhance the fast cornering capability by giving extra tractive power when it is most needed. It also helps in icy or loosely surfaced road conditions for should one wheel lose traction and then suddenly regain it whilst spinning the car could be thrown out of control. Another area in which it tends to help is in starting on slippery surfaces or in accelerating at the car's maximum power, tending to alleviate fish tailing and feed the optimum amount of power for the given surface to the rear wheels. In the opinion of most safety concerned motorists these devices should be standard equipment on all high performance cars.

By adopting the transaxle set up from the 924 complete with the 25mm drive shaft the weight distribution of the car has been kept once more to the almost ideal 49.2% front 50.8% rear. Again the high polar moment of inertia has been sought and obtained, although in early 924's the press and several owners were quick to condemn the gear change for a certain imprecise feeling caused by the length of the gear linkage. This layout has also received some criticism for causing a slightly 'choppy' ride in the 924 although this tendency is noticeably absent from the slightly heavier and more sophisticated 928.

Most Porsches have found praise over the years for superb brakes. Perhaps to further this the factory decided to equip the 944 with all-round internally ventilated discs. Until the advent of the 944 these brakes tended to be the property of a few high speed high priced luxury cars or out and out race or rally cars. Indeed, the very fact that Porsche had used them on the 924 Carrera as a basis for competition homologation showed the care they were taking to bring the car into line with the needs of the sportingly aware motorist. As on the Carrera the discs were of ten inch diameter and assisted by a nine inch servo. As required by several countries they are dual circuit. They are capable, according to the factory, of stopping the car from sixty-two point five miles per hour to a standstill in only 2.9 seconds. In technical terms $9.4 \text{m/s}^2 = 0.96 \text{g}$ (with 55 section tyres on seven inch rims).

As regards cornering the 944 has a lateral acceleration limit of between 0.88 and 0.89g. This speaks volumes for the technicians at Weissach which is credited with the largest and most advanced tyre research drum in Europe. The behaviour of the car at those loadings, however, speaks even more eloquently of the race bred pedigree of every Porsche. To cope with this the rack and pinion steering from the 924 Carrera was adopted and for those who wanted power steering was available as an option, but only on left hand drive cars.

As introduced the car was shod by a choice of rubberwear. In standard guise with light alloy 7×15 rims 185/70 VR 15 CN 36 tyres were offered and drew a luke warm reaction from all who used the car so equipped. The next step consisted of forged alloy rims, $7j \times 15$ front and $8j \times 15$ rear again fitted with CN 36 tyres. The best set up was the $7j \times 16$ forged rims with 205/55 VR 16 ultra low profile tyres. In this guise the press gave their approval.

To take care of the increase in the track the bodywork of the Carrera had been smoothly reworked and at the same time the Porsche stylists had proved that although working to a brief which called for far more contemporary emphasis than they would usually include in their own products they had still managed to evolve a clean and pleasing shape which would stand, with a few alterations, until the car reached the end of its natural product life. As can be seen from the air flow registered in the windtunnel testing the shape is also extremely efficient.

Certain features had been retained from the Carrera, among them the pleasantly functional rear spoiler and the complete absence of brightwork. All in all, however, the car revealed its ancestry while at the same time giving the impression of being a far more purposeful tool and more importantly a further evolution.

The interior of the new car bore the usual family resemblance to its forerunners. Again use has been made of the 911 seats, the company claiming that the seats harmonised with spring rate, anti-roll and damping action to provide the driver with enough feeling for the road conditions to help him stay awake! Perhaps this could be an example of another Porsche first, that of making respectable the art of 'driving by the seat of the pants'. On a more serious level the seat squabs seem to be a fine compromise for very few people of almost any shape or size fail to find the long distance comfort quite exceptional.

As well as providing comfort the seats have also been carefully structured to minimise the risk of submarining, that is sliding from beneath the seat belts, in a high speed crash. The head restraints are integral to the seatbacks which some find uncomfortable but no doubt once again the company has aimed at a form of compromise for the various shapes and heights which they must cater for. The car is fitted with inertia reel belts for the front passengers and lap belts for those small or unlucky enough to occupy the rear. Indeed, with a certain amount of honesty the company brochure refers to the rear seats as being able to accommodate two adults 'on short journeys'. For those who want them a 'sports seat' is available offering a higher degree of lateral support than the standard package.

In the standard package the upholstery is a particularly unappealing plastic material. The brochure points out that the 944's special atmosphere is the result of select materials. In fairness, with the cloth inserts the leatherette is perhaps not quite unbearable but in a car with

The interior could be best described as more functional than luxurious as befits the modern sports car. The main instruments are clear and easy to read while the heater and radio controls fall conveniently to hand. The minor column mounted controls proclaim the original VW Audi design commission, for as in the 924 they come straight from the parts bin of the latter company.

The lack of clearance between the seat squab and steering wheel is noticeable, there is also a lack of rear passenger space.

some pretence to opulence for the middle range executive the standard offering leaves much to be desired even compared to the normal level of interior fitment on the more enlightened Japanese makes. Unfortunately for the person seeking anything approaching the level of trim with which the name Porsche should be synonymous, dipping into the optional extra list is necessary—so you pay the price of indulgence. For the more committed of the Porsche enthusiasts there is always the 'cloth Porsche' choice which has the name of the company running through the weave.

Standard equipment on the 944 Lux includes headlight washers, a night dimming mirror, long range driving lights recessed into the front bumpers which also serve as flashers in daylight conditions when the main lights are retracted, a heated rear screen with wash and wipe, heated interior-adjustable exterior rear view mirrors. The wind tunnel work which went into the exterior and engine bay airflow was also put to good use regarding the interior ventilation which was a source of complaint in the 924. Improvements were made at the same time to the water ducting on the exterior which it would seem have had a beneficial effect on the wind noise levels encountered in high speed cruising.

To satisfy both governments and prospective purchasers the modern sports car must convince from the outset that as well as performance it offers safety. To this end all critical points in the interior are padded, switches are recessed or made from deformable material. An energy absorbent steering column is fitted and all materials are flame retardant. Attention has also been given to the outer areas of the car with a view to minimising injury in the case of pedestrian accidents. The windscreen wiper spindles are recessed below the bonnet, the mirrors swivel upon impact and even when raised the headlamps are carefully rounded to avoid any undue lacerations to the victim.

Although the price structure of the 944 does not allow the composite front and rear crushable areas of the 928, passengers are protected by two large deformable areas front and rear. The bumpers are formed in a polyurethane material (trim) and mounted on shock absorbing tubes to contain smaller impacts. In harder impacts the bonnet crumples in a pre-determined manner, in effect folding back on itself and being caught by arrester-hooks before coming into contact with the windscreen. The connecting tube and drive shaft to the rear transaxle is also cited by the makers as helping distribute shock from a major impact while preventing the engine penetrating the passenger compartment, the same dispersal helping absorb energy from rear end shunts as well.

The normal test for lateral rigidity and door strength in any vehicle is that which came about as a direct result of Ralph Nader's mid sixties campaigns for greater automotive safety. It consists of a ram driving a rigid barrier weighing some 1,800 kilos into the side of the stationary vehicle at twenty miles per hour. This process is supposed to test both rigidity and the ability of the doors to function in heavy side-on accidents. The Porsche 944 as the 924 before it is constructed in such a way that the passenger compartment forms a safety cell. Thus as the car's extremities crumple the rigid framework surrounding the whole passenger compartment remains, in theory, intact. If the tests can be taken as a fair guide line to the behaviour of the car in this type of crash it must be admitted that the 944 passes with flying colours with locks, door frames and the doors themselves standing up to repeated impacts while maintaining full function.

The same design philosophy also maintains rigidity in a roll-over accident. Here the door frames, windscreen surround (and to a certain degree the laminated windscreen itself) and the framework supporting the glass rear hatch combine to form a structure similar to the rally

Just as the initial publicity photography for the 928 featured the car towing a trailer full of hydroplanes, Porsche chose to emphasise the sportive nature of the 944 by incorporating another adventure sport, this time hang gliding was chosen.

driver's roll cage. In the testing required by most governments the doors become subject to tremendous centrifugal force thus the safety locks on all modern cars have to be able to deal with more than just impact. These tests are valid insofar as the inherent safety of all the cars which pass them is very much higher than the vehicles of just a decade or so ago. In the case of parts such as locks it is an illustration of the benefits of the cross fertilisation which took place at the design stage that the expensive and time consuming process of developing or adapting the subsidiary equipment of other manufacturers has been avoided by using the parts already common to the VW and Audi ranges, parts which had already proved more than capable of meeting the stringent regulations imposed by the various standards' authorities around the world.

Obviously fire is another danger when crashes occur. To help guard against this, as well as the flame retardent interior fittings, the fuel tank is deformable to help guard against rupture and spillage. Attention has also been given to the positioning and composition of the petrol lines. In all the whole package adds up to quite an achievement in safety terms for a lightweight fast touring machine such as this.

While considering various engine layouts for the inevitable day when the two litre engine would be no more; Porsche tried at least one other layout insofar as they installed a modified Renault V6. Unlike the De Lorean, however, which was designed to take this bulky unit from day one they found the unit impractical in several ways. The weight worked against them upsetting the perfect balance characteristics of the vehicle, the sheer bulk of the V configuration filled to capacity all the available underbonnet space and perhaps most telling in the long term was the difficulty of maintaining the proper running temperature with this unit.

That the forty five degree engine could be considered a cool running motor is beyond doubt. The ingenious oil/water intercooler and aforementioned improved underbonnet ventilation testifying to the theory of this. The facilities at Weissach could also be said to have contributed to this for here the fifty thousand mile emission tests are carried out by robot drivers who never get bored with driving the cars in the manner laid down by the Federal authorities on the restrictively programmed rolling roads. These same machines can just as easily drive the cars through the arctic test conditions or the baking desert conditions which all reputable development facilities provide. They cannot, however, create the genuine experience of the critical moment which sometimes arises in the most mundane road journeys.

To take advantage of the similarity of the 944 to the 924 Carrera and at the same time place the car in the kind of situations that even the most daring enthusiastic owner would be hard put to emulate, two Austrians Rudi Lins and Gerhard Plattner were entrusted with a pre-production example and given a rather awesome task of testing it over the world's most trying road conditions.

Planning for the trip was given to Plattner who came up with a tour itinerary which would have delighted that pioneer of long distance record making André Citroen. In essence the test was to drive from Europe to Mali via the Sahara desert. Navigate one hundred alpine passes before a high speed dash through the most congested and hectic traffic conditions in Europe in cities as diverse as Hamburg and Rome and finally run the car flat out for three hours on a race track.

The project was sponsored by Mobil partly to promote their Mobil 1 lubricating oil which had just been chosen by Porsche as an acceptable lubricant across its range. The resulting trip featured heavily in the issue of *Christophorus*, the Porsche house magazine, alongside the article which introduced the new car to Porsche fans world wide.

The route taken across the desert was the torturous Tanezrouft track but unlike Citroen who had opted to use this route to publicise his vehicles some forty years earlier the only modification to the standard car was to be a sump guard to ward off the desert stones which can disembowel almost any unprotected vehicle. Further on the route taken into Mali was to be the Rallye Oasis route which had been the proving grounds of the VW Iltis, the all-terrain vehicle which formed the basis for the Audi Quattro.

The car ran faultlessly through this ordeal collecting only minor damage to the front spoiler and needing only new front shock absorbers at the end of the African adventure. In the process the trip proved not only the sound engineering structure of the car but also that the Bosch fuel injection could take the worst conditions of desert dust and tropical humidity without any problem. The worth of the Reynolds block was demonstrated by the fact that the car used only one pint of Mobil 1 in 3016 miles of appalling conditions (a good advertisement for the oil as well) and that the air conditioning supplied as standard on the US models could certainly cope with anything likely to be encountered in the USA.

This endurance run coming as it did after months of intensive testing both in the laboratory and on the roads marked the point at which Porsche introduced the car to the ever eager press. The reaction was ecstatic. In most cases journalists conveniently chose to forget that only the engine was a total Zuffenhausen product as they ran into reams of praise for the 'total Porsche'. One journalist even went so far as to cite the minor equipment switches, lights indicators etc, as the last vestige of Audi. Others took the line that the 924 had finally grown into the kind of car a 'real' Porsche should be. Almost without exception the early reports chose the engine with its balance shafts as the focal point for the main weight of their attention. "But the heart of a sports car remains its engine, and when a company as highly respected as Porsche produces a new power unit it's not an event to be taken lightly." As Rex Greenslade so aptly expressed it in *Motor*.

Most European journalists immediately chose to see the 944 as the model to bridge the gap between the normally aspirated and the turbocharged 924, ignoring the telling fact that VW had already announced that the two litre engine had been superceded in their own range and was thus well on the way to the end of its economic production potential. The US journalists were more specifically briefed by a press release which stated "it was possible to arrange the 944 below the luxury class in price: it fits between the 924 and the 911SC". Even here the message that the 924 Carrera was due to disappear failed to make much impression and the 944 could be said perhaps in the initial road tests to be dogged by performance comparisons to the faster and more expensive Carrera.

Of the publications most involved with the industry it was apparent right from the off that those biased more heavily toward motor sport were those which would take the new Porsche most seriously. Indeed magazines such as *Auto Motor und Sport* in Germany, *Motoring News* and *Motor Sport* in Great Britain with *Road and Track* in the USA really needed a new set of superlatives to describe the car. Without exception all were more than lavish in their commendation and all managed in one way or another to convey the impression that here at last was the front engined vehicle which would not only satisfy the long term Porsche

With the exception of the black energy-absorbing over riders which occupy the space which the European model uses for long distance driving lights the US specification 944 is visually identical to the European model. Performance is also slightly inhibited by the need to incorporate anti-pollution measures with a 0-60 time of 8.3 seconds and top speed of 130 mph.

enthusiast but also win a whole new market sector of sports orientated middle range executive buyers who would previously have been unable to afford the 928, found the 911 too ostentatious or in most guises too expensive and at the same time shunned the 924 as being 'the bargain basement Porsche'.

Various parts of the car came under scrutiny not least the revamped body styling. In every case the reviews were favourable. In particular Alan Henry writing in *Motor Sport* probably came closest to the prevalent mood when he spoke of 'refined unobtrusive effectiveness'. A view reinforced when the doyen of British motoring journalists William Boddy reappraising the car for the same magazine some eleven months later found only the relatively low gearing of the steering to complain of before likening the reputation and products of Porsche within the parameters of their chosen market to that of Rolls Royce in theirs.

A point many technically orientated writers chose to pick up was the bottom end of the engine. As has already been stated the designers were constrained, in the interests of production economy and efficiency to utilise the equipment already to hand in the factory. This led to including an interesting ladder type of arrangement securing the crankshaft with its five main bearings to the block. An arrangement such as this had been used in the all-conquering Ford Cosworth Grand Prix engine but with the exception of the road going Lotus sixteen valve engine Porsche were the first to see the advantages of this method for maximising the exceptional rigidity inherent in their light alloy block with this weight saving and from a servicing point of view, convenient method of carrying the main bearing caps.

Another area which the international press were very quick to seize upon was the clearance between front seat squab and steering wheel rim. Not only is this limited whilst the car is parked and the wheels in the straight ahead position, the fact that the steering wheel rim is slightly eccentric can make the positioning extremely irritating if not positively annoying in everyday use for those with longer than average (whatever that may mean) legs. This was a fault that had been transferred completely unmodified from the 924 and one which seems totally trivial in terms of work effort to correct.

Almost all journalists had praise for the flat torque characteristics of the car, John Miles writing in *Autocar* proclaiming the engine as 'an absolute honey. It responds beautifully from 1,500rpm upwards, and from 2,500rpm onwards there is real acceleration on tap'. Unlike Boddy, however, Miles thought the slightly higher gearing of the steering actually enhanced the feel of the car, a view shared by the majority of Continental commentators.

Although Porsche claimed a ten percent efficiency increase in the interior ventilation most scribes found this hard to credit although in fairness most pointed out that some discernable improvement was there. Many felt that the air conditioning which was standard on all US spec cars should have been standardised on the European model as well as has been the case in recent years with Lotus.

Another area which came in for criticism from more discerning writers was that of braking. Whilst no-one actually stated baldly that the brakes were anything but good almost unanimously the servo and the general lack of precise feel for the brakes came in for its share of questioning. The language used varied in force from mild warnings to beware of heavy or late braking in the wet to statements to the effect that it was 'over servoed'. Few American testers chose to complain but it must be borne in mind that at the beginning of its career the 924 had been constantly criticised by the US motoring press for the fade characteristics in its disc/drum set up. While America is burdened with its ridiculous fifty five mph limit coast to coast it still seems that those who buy Porsches want to know that they can travel at nearly three times this slow pace and stop in comfort and safety.

While on the subject of the braking perhaps here it would be interesting to note that the only really abrasive trade report on the car, and the one which comes from the most independently minded magazine, that of L. J. K. Setright for *Car*, found the softness of the pedal made the braking difficult to modulate. The report also pointed out to those who were not familiar with the front engine rear gearbox layout the pitfalls of fast cornering in this type of car.

The crux of this is that the weight distribution although making possible the relatively high levels of cornering adhesion in normal usage made the car very quick to yaw when the limit is reached. The fact that it is quick to recover is also pointed out but of more interest is the imparted knowledge that the behavious of the car in a yaw is bound to be reproduced in pitching motions. Thus although at normal road speeds only a basic level of competence would be required to exact the best from the car a yawing fit at high speed could require a certain amount of expertise to control especially if variations in pitch were taken into account.

Perhaps alone among the international cognoscenti who hailed the new car Setright refused to categorise the car except to speak of it as a fast and sleek boulevardier. He gives credit where due to the engine road holding and ride, although qualifying the second somewhat by drawing attention to the superiority of the ultra low profile Dunlop D4 tyres over the standard equipment Pirelli CN 36. His praise was also fulsome on the economy and the driving position yet once again the steering is singled out for a good dose of vitriol. In his own words; 'Most miserably inadequate of all is the steering. For a sports car, even for a high performance saloon, even for a Los Angeles boulevardier, it is preposterously low geared.'

Once more the ventilation is the subject of some criticism but the report ends on an extremely positive note with Setright choosing to point out what so many had said on the introduction of the 924; that the essence of any Porsche lay in development and this being the case the wealth of uncritical adulation which had greeted this particular one having assured it of commercial success the car would one day reach a point of development at which it became tolerable. Once tolerable, ran his rationale, the car would be immediately unexceptionable which in terms of vehicles past and present would probably make it unique.

In the USA such press criticism that the car attracted was confined to the need to 'optionalise' the car to get the best from it. Although such features as air conditioning, electric windows, tinted glass, cassette holder and the normal front anti-roll bar were carried as standard fittings that country had grown used to the comprehensive packaging of such lavishly equipped cars as the Datsun 260Z and the Mazda RX 7. To have to pay for such items as cruise control, digital cassette radio, rear wiper and automatic transmission seemed out of keeping with the car's image. Further to actually make the car perform in the manner that most enthusiasts would want they would have to go shopping through the sports options packages available for such items as sport shocks, uprated anti-roll bars, ultra low profile tyres in sixteen inch rims, sports seats, limited slip differential etc. Even such niceties as the headlight washers and the side mouldings were placed on the option list as was the painting of the alloy wheel centres to white or platinum.

Such was the acceptance of the car, however, that by the end of 1983, with power steering added to the list of standard equipment, the US Porsche Audi distributorship was citing the sales success of the 944 as a major factor in achieving record sales the previous year.

Additions to the basic equipment of the car have been made since its introduction. Notable amongst them are the econometer and brake pad wear warning light on the dashboard which were first seen in 1982. Twin vanity mirrors and an electrically operated tilting removeable glass sunroof replacing the earlier item were added in 1983 as was a new National Panasonic radio and cassette system which remains exclusive to Porsche. Not perhaps the detail modifications which most owners and journalists would have liked to see but the recipe of the car was so clearly successful at the introduction that the factory must be loath to spend time and effort on increasing such things as brake sensitivity, interior ventilation and the amount of space between the steering wheel and the seat squab.

At the time of writing some thirty thousand 944s have found owners and the waiting list for the car still brings a warm glow to the hearts of the marketing men in Zuffenhausen. As predicted the car has achieved the sort of classless acceptability of such devices as the Mini Cooper, the Renault Five or the MGB in their heyday. Some measure of the car's on-going viability can be gained by the editorial accorded to it in the March 84 edition of *Fast Lane* magazine where editor Peter Dron writes: "Our Porsche 944 is due to arrive soon. We were very keen to obtain one, as we regard it as one of the most important sports car designs to appear in recent years . . . (The 944) is a mobile tribute to Porsche's acknowledged prowess in engineering development . . . possibly not only the Porsche of the future, but points the way for other manufacturers. We can hardly wait to get our hands on it."

The press shop at Neckarsulm. Here the body panels take shape from treated sheet steel. Sides, roof, floor pan and bulkheads are formed on these presses the size of which can be judged by the figures in the background in picture.

Another shot of the press shop with trolley carrying sheet steel in centre.

Rollers feed the galvanised sheet steel to the robot (centre left) which services the press.

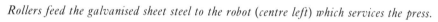

An overhead conveyor takes 944 front wings from the press shop to the body fabrication plant.

Smaller frame parts being stamped out by skilled operators.

Fabricated body shells emerging from the cataphoretic paint process by another overhead conveyor.

The primed shell being lifted from the conveyor to meet its own particular trolley.

The next stage and the shells are transferred to a ground drag line en route to the first stages of production.

A bodyshell waits to be examined for small flaws.

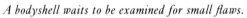

Hand painted shells emerging from the spray booth.

Once wired exterior fittings are added.

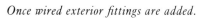

Electrical systems are installed.

Painted shells en route to final assembly.

Exterior fittings now in place the car is prepared for engine and drivetrain installation.

A fully assembled engine and drivetrain waits on its trolley for installation.

In one simple operation the whole installation of engine and drive train.

The operation done the trolley retracts and is ready to accept another engine drivetrain package.

Ingenious split level line allows simultaneous installation of interior trim, glass and brakes.

Door and hatchback seals being installed.

Locks being fitted.

Last adjustments and checks.

All reservoirs ready to be filled.

Now complete the cars are carried into the inspection zone where any last minute adjustments can be made before dispatching another beautifully made car to its waiting owner.

Part 4

The Driver's View

My first aquaintance with the Porsche 944 was under somewhat exotic circumstances. The example in question was a veritable symphony in pearlescent white which Alan Giddings, the Porsche agent in Bahrein had ordered on behalf of a customer and pressed into service upon delivery as his personal transport. As these things go it was a fairly uncomfortable meeting, the roads of the island and the lack of rear seat space rendered all but the smooth way in which the car navigated the Corniche a bone crushing torture.

Selling motor cars to the arabs has always had its quirky side and the week previously I had been hearing of the trials and tribulations of the Porsche agent in the richest of all arabian cities, Riyadh, who had lost credibility totally in the arab section of his market when a 928 which had been carrying a fourteen year old prince was displayed at the annual 'Motor Week'. In fact the remains of the car were strung between two posts and the only features which helped identify the mess as a vehicle were the somewhat distorted wheels. Unfortunately for the prince, his chauffeur and the luckless Porsche dealer the car was unable to survive being driven into the parapet of a bridge at nearly maximum speed. The incident had resulted in the car taking the maximum share of the blame rather than the driver, who it was reliably whispered about, had been the royal sibling and as such above the suspicion of careless driving.

This was probably the reason that there was no 944 at that year's Saudi show although the right-hand drive version had gone on sale in the UK some three months earlier and the first few examples were showing themselves on the Autobahns in Germany. Even so the car was rare enough for one to believe that the factory had stopped production a few days after the initial announcement. Thus the ride in the Bahrain car was the first real close up to come my way and left a lasting impression both for the smoothness of the engine and the smallmess of the passenger accommodation.

'So what's it like?' I asked Alan.

'To be honest,' He replied, 'it's the first Porsche I've ever known to handle like a Lotus.'

Praise indeed from the informed, for at the time Mr Giddings was one of the few people in the world to hold both Porsche and Lotus franchises. Even allowing for the fact that when the word Lotus is mentioned all those individuals who have ever aspired to the pole at Monaco get misty eyed at the thought of a Europa, Elan or Esprit on a winding road, Lotus is still the yardstick by which the behaviour of any inferior sporting carriage is judged in the handling stakes.

The next time a 944 came my way for any length of time was in Qatar where an arab friend was kind enough to lend me his newly delivered example for a quick trip from the Sheraton, Doha into the city itself. In the half hour or so in which the car was in my charge it convinced me that although the Lotus comparison was somewhat overstated Mr Giddings had been right in his opinion that the 944 was a born winner. Over the mixture of road surfaces in Qatar the car behaved impeccably even though some were little better than builders tracks, whilst on the Corniche which led to the hotel the rev limiter cut in in second gear to emphasise just how smooth and free revving the big four really is.

Half an hour is hardly time to assimilate more than a few basics with any car and apart from the smoothness of the engine and the quick and efficient way in which the air conditioning neutralised the blistering heat the main thoughts which remained as I handed the car back was that the tape player was not up the standard of the rest of the package. A feeling obviously shared by the people responsible for these things at Porsche for they changed soon after to the National Panasonic set up currently on offer.

Indeed it was only when this book was first mooted and Porsche Great Britain were kind enough to lend me the example which graces the front cover that I really began to take a serious interest in the beast. As such it is a vehicle which totally repays serious consideration.

A maxim amongst motoring journalists has long been 'what looks right usually is right.' From this standpoint very few cars can ever have been 'righter' than the 944. Even on first glance the car gives a wonderful impression of speed and proportion. Gone is the slightly fragile, skinny wheeled look of the 924 and the resultant improvements have left a car that stylistically stands with almost any other in its class. Indeed, if one compares the 944 to its two most obvious rivals in the USA, i.e., the Datsun 300 ZX and the Mazda RX7 its classic European lines tend to make the former look over Americanised and grossly out of proportion and the latter appear some kind of clumsy copy, not quite elegant enough to conquer anything except the market which demands a sports car for the sake of long lost virility.

The interior is perhaps the most basic aspect of the whole car. Not because it lacks the detail finish of the rest of the vehicle but more that it is extremely well finished, a credit in fact to the men who build it, but somehow characterless. The front seats are adequate, although for some the integral headrests are positioned somewhat inconveniently. The sports seats are marginally more comfortable than the standard items on longer runs and give more lateral support. Fore and aft adjustment is

With headlights raised none of the grace is lost. The lights raise and lower with commendable speed and in case of malfunction the 'flasher' lever works on the long distance lamps in the front bumper.

The neatly finished cockpit of 94 FOR with its elegant pinstriping, leather bound steering wheel and gear lever and the well laid-out fascia.

adequate for my height (six foot two) although with the seat comfortably back the gear lever is perhaps an inch or so too far forward in the upper half of the grid to be really easy to hand. The same also applying to the heater and radio controls.

Annoyingly the car does not come fitted with the air conditioning which has become de rigeur in the States and is sported as standard equipment by both the rivals mentioned earlier. Another annoyance is the positioning of the steering wheel which for some reason best known to the makers is still not adjustable. The result of this is that one has the choice of either steering with ones fingertips or squeezing ones legs up behind the wheel which although bringing all the ancillary equipment back within easy reach makes long journeys tedious for those prone to cramp.

Much consideration has gone into the positioning of the pedals and a thoughtful touch is a comfortable pad by the clutch on which to rest the unemployed foot. The major instruments are well layed out for any but the tallest driver, each being easily read and exceptionally well illuminated for night driving. The lesser instruments such as oil

Probably the single most irritating aspect for the driver is the lack of space between the steering wheel and the seat squab necessitating this type of 'knees akimbo' style of driving.

pressure guage, ammeter and brake pad wear warning lamp are situated along with a clock in the centre consol above the heater controls which in turn are mounted above the stereo radio cassette. The minor controls will be familiar to anyone who has driven an Audi for they are common to the whole of the upper end of the VAG network and uniformly excellent.

It is the engine, however, which really draws comment with the 944. Somehow this unit seems to embody the whole design and development policy of the house of Porsche. To the technical writers it was almost too good to be true, its unique configuration and dimensions allowing them to burble gloriously of 'ample squish' and 'maximum lean running of some seventeen to one'. Even the meticulous casting temperature of 1470 degrees Fahrenheit under seven point one pounds per square inch pressure in injection served steel moulds was quoted more than once.

The difficulty involved in maintaining the same expansional coefficient between block and pistons was justly highlighted by some whilst others marvelled at the integrally cast, rather than drilled, oil passages. For those older scribes who delight in drawing parallels between ancient and modern it was a welcome opportunity to recall the magnificent early twenties three litre W. O. Bentleys. To all the counter rotating shafts were an object of supreme fascination. In short the half V8, which had been turned into a unique four, represents both shrewd forward planning from the engineering department and cost saving efficiency in production, policies always adhered to by the Zuffenhausen family.

Starting the car was interesting for this engine hums into life rather than bursts or throbs. In the case of 94 FOR the next two minutes were to be the only fraught ones of the whole test for it was parked directly beneath the wide windows of Porches UK headquarters and neatly hemmed in by other desirable and expensive machinery. One shudders to think of the reputation of anyone scraping paintwork on such cars before leaving the car park. The resulting manoeuvres were carried out with the type of consideration more normally reserved for those occasions when one finds oneself carrying a tray of crystal glass through a crowded party.

Once on the road and London bound the car really began to come into its own. Immediate impressions were of a car in which nothing needed to be hurried. The gear shift felt firm and positive, totally adequate yet lacking the direct feel of certain competitors. The clutch is heavy with a fairly long travel and takes a little time to get used to. The feeling of always having to change gear with ones knees spread apart to avoid the steering wheel can be disconcerting and yet soon becomes a part of the automatic adjustment that one must make for any new vehicle. In short the car gave a superb feeling of unruffled confidence, a marvellous first road impression for any type of car.

Mid afternoon on a Friday is certainly not the best time to try crossing London in an unfamiliar car. However, it seems as good a test of the car in traffic as any so after about half an hour's cruising on the M4 some two and a quarter hours were taken in reaching the M11. In traffic the real inconvenience of the instrumentation manifested. As mentioned before the yellow figured instrumentation is extremely straightforward and easy to read with the exception of the temperature guage which for anyone over five foot seven must be almost permanently obscured by the steering wheel rim. Not that this was needed on this particular occasion for the needle stayed rock steady half way across its sweep regardless of the nose to tail crawling in the seventy degree spring sunshine.

The time spent in this traffic also served to good purpose insofar that it gave time to acclimatise to the somewhat imprecise feeling of the clutch. It also reminded me that anyone who drives a new Porsche of any type is the object of a certain amount of scrutiny from fellow road users. Everyone seems to be keen to see just what type of driver has paid in excess of fifteen thousand pounds for this four wheeled monument to self indulgence.

On motorways the car is almost impossible to keep below the legal limit. The smooth way in which the power goes down onto the road. The lack of wind and engine noise at high cruising speeds and the odd sight of the econometer at the top of the rev counter reading just over thirty five miles to the gallon at some ninety five miles per hour all conspire to make a mockery of Britain's seventy miles per hour limit. Only the rumble of the road surface and the thumping noise as the wheels negotiate some irregularity in the tarmac give any indication of quickness in this car.

So smooth is the engine that the car maintains a deceptively slow feel even under the most vigorous acceleration. The lack of fuss with which the forged alloy wheels with their low-profile tyres transmit the power to the road leaves one wondering whether ones driving technique is lacking until one looks at times elapsed to various speeds. This makes the car extremely flattering to the smoother driver. It also has the effect of seemingly shrinking familiar journeys while demanding far less effort and inflicting far less nervous strain than any other car in its class.

In effect the car is built for cruising. It is superb in situations where there is need for only two people to be accommodated and a lot of ground has to be covered. As such it falls short of being a Grand Tourer for such cars by the nature of the name must be able to carry at least four in comfort and enough luggage to make a grand tour a realistic possibility.

Although it certainly does not seem to be welded to the road in the way that Lotus and the finer Maseratti and smaller Ferrari's are the road holding is truly excellent. Originally road tester's tended to speak of the car tucking in on fast cornering. This is certainly not true of the car tested here at any normal or indeed slightly abnormal cross country speeds. Only when negotiating certain roundabouts against the normal camber did the car even begin to feel that it could give problems and

Rear view of 94 FOR shows clearly the electric tilt sunroof in its raised position and the oddly placed (for the British driver) rear screen wiper.

very few owners should ever find themselves in this rather contrived situation at significant speed.

The almost equal weight distribution allows the full sure footedness of today's tyres to be exploited. Over twisting country roads only the driver's nerve can be said to govern the speed of progress for as one 944 owner put it to me 'it seems that I would have to do something incredibly stupid to force the car into a bad mistake'. Changes in camber, potholes, tractors pulling out of side turnings or badgers crossing the road. All occured when the car was under test and nothing phased the handling at all. Even allowing for the April weather with its occasional downpours the time spent with 94 FOR must rank as some of the most pleasant the author can recall.

Only the brakes led to some misgiving's and these were soon dispelled. On wet roads it seems that one only has to exceed the pressure needed by a fraction to lock up the front wheels. Once again practice makes perfect and it would be churlish to suggest that this fault cannot be discounted for only extreme clumsiness could cause this to become a

124

real danger. Far more of a problem in the wet could be that the magnificent handling could lead to over-confidence and in turn to underestimating the movements of others. On more than one occasion on a wet motorway I found myself having to take violent evasive action as someone pulled out into my path or underestimated my speed of approach. Each time I found the car perfectly able to cope.

One bone of contention that arose from wet weather driving was that the Germans had left the rear screen wiper, a bothersome device which intrudes into the luggage space, on the left hand side of the car thus restricting the right hand drivers rearward view in bad weather. Also this inadequate device has no intermittent wipe and is irritatingly noisy. The windshield wipers and washers are more than adequate although the headlight washers seemed unable to do more than lubricate the mixture of dust and dead insects which build up in fast night driving.

As benefits a car which in its native country must deal with some of the hardest winter conditions anywhere in the world the demisting system is superb with a little graphic guide to full demist actually printed on the heater controls. This little idiot pointer also gives some indication of the trouble Porsche take in making sure that the owner always knows how to get the best from his car. While most other manufacturers are content with including a simple instruction booklet Porsche throw in a small library neatly packed in a small plastic wallet.

Demisting apart the heating and ventilation system is certainly not as refined as one would have expected. The heater controls make it extremely difficult to obtain just the right temperature and the lack of any efficient ram effect at speeds under those of motorway cruising mean that the fan has to be utilised at round-town speeds. Admittedly the electrically tilting sunroof makes a pleasant throughput of air easier to obtain but delightful as this is it can be impractical in wet weather.

Of the other equipment the stereo system deserves a measure of praise for it is both easy to tune and programme, with the on/off volume control also doubling as the activator for the self-seeking mechanism, and gives good reproduction from its four small speakers. Also included is a front to rear balance control which apart from saving anyone unfortunate enough to be riding in the rear from deafness also helps combat rearward distraction in the case of driver fatigue.

Over all the quality of the electrical fittings leaves nothing to be

Rear stowage space is increased to some degree by this locker at the left of the rear of the car.

With the emergency rear seats folded forward loading space is increased fairly substantially.

desired. The windows and mirrors are electric of course and the adjustment for both mirrors falls easily to hand whilst in motion. The electric tilt roof works at the touch of a button beside the stereo, a boon when anyone chooses to smoke in the car. For smokers an ashtray is provided in the centre consol but for the driver it involves some contortion to use it.

These levels of comfort coupled with the lack of wind and engine noise would have been an anathema to the traditional sports car buff. In fact the whole package with its precise steering, which although power assisted gives ample road feel, predictable handling and overall air of unassuming efficiency is as far removed from the crudity of yesterday as is Concorde from the DC3. Admittedly the old style sports car pilot would have been at home with the stubby gearshift and leather bound wheel but the car has never been sold as cult car for those who believe that the age of the sports car ended with the pull up hood or the heater as standard equipment.

Without doubt the car is fun but it is not the car which the would be Grand Prix pilot or top international rally ace is going to be able to take out into the country and perfect handbrake turns or opposite locking techniques on. For a start it is too expensive but more importantly it is a car which thrives on being driven smoothly and precisely. A car which prefers to go round bends with all four wheels on the ground. It is certainly not a car in the same mould as the old MGB or the smaller BMWs where the best way around any corner was to hang the back out before catching it on the throttle in mid-slide. The high polar moment of inertia makes it late to break away but it also makes it difficult to recover so its quickest course will always be the neatest one.

Even without these lurid methods of transit the 944 will probably attain the same sort of cult status as the other cars mentioned, for as well as representing the latest thinking in terms of high speed safety, it has that indefinable magic which the name Porsche seems to bring to every car it graces.

Few other companies world-wide can make an artifact desirable simply by adding their trademark. With Porsche it has occasionally worked against them, for instance how much warmer would the reception of the 924 have been if it had worn the four rings of Audi rather than the Porsche shield? The reality is that the motoring public has become so conditioned to equating Porsche with excellence that when Ferdinand Porsche started putting the company name upon articles more usually found in chic boutiques than car showrooms, the artifacts took on a whole charisma ready created by the image of the name.

Not all Porsche owners will readily pay twice the realistic market value for a pair of sunglasses bearing the name Porsche, or for a military style chronometer complete with a compass that they will never use, but there were enough willing to do so to make the Porsche Design range de rigeur among a section of international high society. So successful has this range of merchandise become that the factory now has to maintain a careful watch in world markets against piracy. Even so a great many people who sport Porsche Design cigarette lighters and leather goods do so because they feel they add some flair to their lives although the cars themselves may be way beyond their budgets.

It is perhaps this mystique which will establish the 944 as the classic it will undoubtedly become. In 1983 some sixty per cent of British customers for the 944 were buying their first ever Porsche. The balance was made up from those who had already owned a 924. Admittedly the picture might have been very different if Leyland had carried through their plans to market the fabulous TR8 but even so a fair percentage of these owners would still have been swayed to the Zuffenhausen product by its enviable heritage.

Not that the heritage is only to be found in terms of product image for as more than one eminent motoring writer has observed, the 944 may have been designed by computer but it was refined by men with the race tracks in their blood. This fact becomes more obvious the more one encounters the car. The hours spent on the test track at Weissach and pounding around the Le Mans circuit have left the car as near to perfection as most demanding drivers will ever experience.

Obviously the car has rivals. The two Japanese contenders mentioned earlier in the chapter in the US market for instance. More serious challengers must include the Alpine A310 from the Renault stable and the superb Lotus Excel. Both cars offer the same type of exclusivity backed by Grand Prix pedigree and in the case of Lotus a vastly improved record for quality.

Another rival which is perhaps nearer in spirit is the Alfa Romeo

The rear luggage cover works on the principle of a window blind, here it is seen with the emergency rear seat upright . . .

. . . and here with the seats folded.

GTV6. Like the 944 it carries a two point five litre engine at the front and a five speed gearbox in unit with the rear differential. Performance figures for the two cars are remarkably similar although the Porsche wins out when it comes to fuel economy, the accommodation for the rear passengers is substantially more roomy in the Alfa as it is in the Excel, but the poor record that the Italian cars have displayed when it comes to corrosion plus the rather awkward driving position tends to leave the Porsche at the head of its class as an all round practical and sporting proposition.

Of the other likely rivals in the field some thought must surely be given to the very much more expensive Audi Quattro. There can be little doubt that when it was announced the four wheel drive car from Ingolstadt created tension in all sporting manufacturers circles. So much so that Porsche themselves have announced a four wheel drive 911 variant to compete against it in the Group B category in international rallying. Indeed, comparisons between the Quattro and other sports cars must tend to highlight the gulf in the motor industry's ideals of what actually constitutes a sports car.

The Quattro is a direct derivative of a production saloon carefully modified and hand built to give the type of performance which amply justifies its title of super car. It does, however, rely heavily upon turbo charging and four wheel drive to achieve these ends while as yet neither performance aid has found its way onto the 944 in production form. As benefits its production history the accommodation in the Quattro is more akin to a saloon car than a sports model and this tends to take it out of the direct rival category, yet in terms of desirability the Quattro must surely rank as a rival to the extremely discerning performance orientated motorist. Those younger family men who tire of forcing children, dogs or the occasional full size passengers into the back of the Porsche could well be swayed to find the few extra thousand that the purchase of the Quattro involves.

Of the specialist manufacturers perhaps only TVR with their Tasmin 2+2 can claim to challenge Porsche on both the handling and quality front and, in Britain at least, the car costs roughly the same while offering lower servicing costs due to the use of proprietry parts readily and cheaply available from most Ford or Leyland main agents. Beautiful and wonderfully built as it is, however, the TVR output across the range is extremely small compared to the production of Porsche and this must tell against the car in all important export markets.

This then is 944 as it stands at the time of writing. A car with a select and charismatic appeal which is winning a substantial number of new converts to the Porsche way of driving. Its rivals are also an extremely select set and it is a measure of the integrity of the men behind the scenes at Porsche and their devotion to their concept of what constitutes the perfect sporting compromise that it is so successful.

The rationale behind any car these days is to stay within the realms of current and future automotive legislation whilst offering the customer the optimum available performance within the economic category he chooses to drive in. For major manufacturers the challenge of keeping pace with the legislators and the fashion whims of the prospective customer are purely a matter of mass production economics, and like those men who at the other end of the scale seek desperately for success on the racetracks of the world, they tend to copy each other slavishly.

The compromise that Porsche must make is therefore doubled. Not only do they have to produce a car which has immediate market appeal and can provide the style of motoring which devotees expect but they must also produce a car which will allow development with a minimum of investment to prolong that market appeal far beyond the lifespan of any comparable product from the major manufacturers.

In an age where international market demands are rapidly eroding the nationalistic differences between motor cars; where quality, styling, handling and optional equipment are uniform whether the car in question emanates from Stuttgart, Solihull, Detroit or Okinawa, Porsche are still mastering the art of compromise. The 924 was a valid and worthwhile exercise for the man in the street. The expert and the newly familiarised driver decided that the chassis was underpowered. Porsche provided the 924 Turbo, giving the model not only a new market niche but a whole new sector of market appeal. The 944 is a logical progression offering most of the worthwhile traits of the 924 Turbo with few of its inherent complexities. The next logical step must surely be the 944 Turbo.

The car is expected in the latter half of 1984. Already the Porsche watchers among the motoring fraternity are hazarding more or less informed guesses on the final specification of this car. The favourite opinion seems to be that it will reflect the technology already pioneered in the 924 Turbo with a small KKK turbocharger downstream of the manifold in such a position that the platinum oxygen sensor will remain unaffected and will blow with a maximum boost of a moderate 11 lbs psi giving a useful 200 plus bhp.

The chassis can certainly cope with this increase in power for it will only serve to make the car even more flexible and trauma free in overtaking and mid range acceleration. The market will certainly absorb such production which becomes available and the sensation of the launch will probably cover the demise of the 924.

This is, of course, all conjecture. Either way the compromise will have reached its ultimate format. One is then left wondering what the technical magicians from Zuffenhausen will find to replace the 944 in the middle market range. Notwithstanding the gradual dissipation of fossil fuels and the general levelling of middle class incomes on a world wide scale, one can only hope that the next car will be as pleasant and as practical for its time as the 944 is to ours.

TECHNICAL DATA

Porsche 944 Lux–British Specification 1984

Bodywork	Two-door, 2+2 coupé body, rear window hatch
Engine	Four-cylinder, four-stroke, in-line engine water-cooled, overhead cam-shaft driven by cog belt, two contra-rotating balance shafts to balance masses.
Bore	100mm/3.94in
Stroke	78.9mm/3.11in
Capacity	2479cc/151in³
Compression	10.6:1
Engine output	120kW at 5800rpm (163hp DIN)
Maximum torque	205Nm at 3000rpm (20.9mkp or 151.2lb-ft)
Drive line	Transaxle unit with front mounted engine and rear gearbox, bolted into a rigid drive unit by a connecting tube
Brakes	Dual-circuit hydraulic brake system, inner-vented disc brakes with floating saddles front and rear, brake servo
Weights	DIN empty weight 1180kg/2600lb Permitted total weight 1500kg/3310lb

Performance	Acceleration from 0-100kph (0-62mph) in 8.4 seconds Top speed 220kph or 137mph
Fuel consumption tests (5-speed manual)	Simulated urban driving 24.8mpg
Passenger Car Fuel Consumption Order 1977	Constant speed driving 40.4 mpg 90kph (56mph) Constant speed driving 32.5mpg 120kph (75mph)
Dimensions	Length 4200mm Width 1735mm Height 1275mm Wheelbase 2400mm Front track 1477mm Rear track 1451mm

Technical Data Porsche 944
Original German Specification

Chassis

Bodywork	2-door, 2+2 seat, coupé body, rear hatch
Frame	Unitary steel body, bolt-on front fenders
Front suspension	Independent suspension by transverse links and spring legs (McPherson)
Rear suspension	Independent suspension by semi-trailing arms
Springs and shocks, front	Coil springs (coaxial) with double hydraulic shock legs
Springs and shocks, rear	Transverse torsion bars with double acting hydraulic shock absorbers
Anti-roll bars	Front: 20mm/0.8in rear: 14mm/0.6in
Steering	Rack and pinion, ratio 22.39:1
Brakes	Dual-circuit hydraulic brake system, brake servo, inner-vented disc brakes front and rear, floating calipers
Wheels	7J × 15 pressure-cast aluminium rims Optionally: 7J × 16 forged light alloy rims
Tires	Standard: 185/70 VR 15 Optionally: 205/55 VR 16
Drive train	Transaxle unit with engine in front, gearbox in the rear, bolted together into rigid drive unit by means of connecting tube
	Torsionally elastic (25mm/1in) drive shaft in four bearings, to gearbox in unit with differential, dual-joint shafts with length compensating to rear wheels

Clutch	Single-plate, dry clutch
Gearbox	Fully-synchronised manual gearbox at the rear axle, in one housing with differential, central shift lever on tunnel
	Ratios: 1st gear/i=3.6000 10/36 2nd gear/i =2.1250 16/34 3rd gear/i=1.4583 24/35 4th gear/i=1.0714 28/30 5th gear/i=0.8285 35/29 Final drive/i=3.8888 9/35
Engine	Four-cylinder, four-stroke, inline engine, water cooled, belt-driven overhead camshaft, two balance shafts to control inertial forces
Bore	100mm
Stroke	78.9mm
Capacity	2479cc
Compression ratio	10.6:1
Engine output	120kW DIN at 5800rpm (163.2HP)
Max torque	205Nm at 3000rpm (20.9Kpm/151.2 lb-ft)
Crankshaft	Forged steel, five plain bearings
Valve arrangement	Hanging, in a row
Valve drive	Overhead camshaft and hydraulic tappets
Camshaft drive	By cogged belt
Lubrication	Pressure lubrication with crescent pump
Oil filter	In main stream

Technical Data Porsche 944—(original German specification)

Mixture preparation	Bosch L–Jetronic
Fuel delivery	Electric fuel pump
Octane requirements	98 RON/88 MON
Electrical system	Battery 12V 45Ah
	1260 Watt/90A alternator
Dimensions	Wheelbase 2400mm Front track 1477mm Rear track 1451mm Length 4200mm Width 1735mm Height 1275mm
Liquid capacities	Fuel tank approx. 62 l, 5 as reserve Engine oil 5.5 l Engine coolant 7.0 l Gearbox oil 2.6 l Brake fluid reservoir 0.2 l Windshield and headlight cleaner reservoir, approx. 6.4 l
Weights	DIN empty 1180kg permit total 1500kg
Performance	Acceleration, 0–100km/h: Manual gearbox 8.4 seconds Automatic 9.6 seconds 1km, standing start 29.0 seconds Top Speed 220km/h
Fuel consumption	7.0 l at 90km/h 8.7 l at 120km/h 11.4 l on urban cycle

1984 US Specifications

Engine	4-cylinder, in-line
Bore	100mm (3.94in.)
Stroke	78.9mm (3.11in.)
Displacement	2479cc (151cu.in.)
Compression ratio	9.5:1
Horsepower (SAE Net)	143 at 5500rpm
Max. torque (SAE Net)	137 ft. lbs at 3000rpm

Engine design

Engine block	Silicon-aluminum alloy
Crankshaft	Forged steel, 5 main bearings; two balance shafts
Connecting rods	Sintered steel
Pistons	Cast aluminum, iron-coated
Cylinder head	Aluminum alloy 'cross-flow' design
Valve train	Overhead camshaft, belt-driven; hydraulic lifters
Cooling system	Water-cooled, thermostatically controlled electric fan
Lubrication system	Sickle-gear pump, crankshaft-driven
Fuel injection	Electronic w/oxygen sensor (DME)

Electrical system

Battery	12V/63 Amp.h
Alternator	1260 watts/90 amp.
Ignition	Electronic (DME)

Drive train	Rigid driveshaft tube connecting front engine and rear transmission
Driveshaft diameter	25mm
Clutch	Single dry plate; hydraulic operation, self-adjusting

Technical specifications—1984 US Specifications—continued

Transmission	Manual	Automatic
Gear ratios: 1st	3.60	2.71
2nd	2.13	1.50
3rd	1.46	1.00
4th	1.07	—
5th	0.73	—
Final Drive	3.89	3.45
Reverse	3.50	2.43

Body and Frame Galvanised steel, unitized construction
Drag coefficient   .35

Suspension   Fully independent
Front   MacPherson struts w/coil springs, 20mm
        stabilizer bar (21.5mm optional)
Rear   Diagonal arms, transverse torsion bars;
        (14mm stabilizer bar optional)

Steering   Rack and pinion, power-assisted
Ratio   18.5:1
Turns (lock-to-lock)   3.1
Turning circle (curb to   31.2ft.
curb)

Wheels $7J \times 15$ cast alloy (optional forged alloy:
        $7J \times 15$ front, $8J \times 15$ rear)

Tires   215/60 VR steel-belted

Brakes   Four-wheel ventilated discs; power assisted
Disc diameter   282mm front, 289mm rear

Technical specifications—1984 US specifications—continued

Capacities

Engine oil	5.3 quarts
Engine coolant	9.0 quarts
Transmission/ differential	5.5 pints
Fuel tank	17.4 gallons
Windshield washer tank	6.9 quarts

Dimensions

Wheelbase	94.5in
Track: front	58.2in
rear	57.1in
Length	168.9in
Width	68.3in
Height (unloaded)	50.2in
Ground clearance (loaded)	4.9in
Weight	2778lbs

Performance:	Manual	Automatic
0–50mph	5.9 seconds	6.4 seconds
0–60mph	8.3 seconds	9.8 seconds
Top speed	130mph	130mph
Fuel economy	22	21
(city/highway)	35	29
	26	24
49 States	22/35 mpg	21/29mpg
California	21/34mpg	20/27mpg

Technical Data

Chassis

Bodywork	2-door, 2 + 2-seat coupé body, rear hatch
Frame	Unitary steel body, bolt-on front fenders
Front suspension	Independent suspension by transverse links and spring legs (McPherson)
Rear suspension	Independent suspension by semi-trailing arms
Springs and shocks, front	Coil springs (coaxial) with double acting hydraulic shock legs
Springs and shocks, rear	Transverse torsion bars with double acting hydraulic shock absorbers
Anti-roll bars	Front: 20 mm/0.8 in – rear: 14 mm/0.6 in
Steering	Rack and pinion, ratio 22.39 : 1
Brakes	Dual-circuit hydraulic brake system, brake servo, inner-vented disc brakes front and rear, floating calipers
Wheels	7 J x 15 pressure-cast aluminum rims Optionally: 7 J x 16 forged light alloy rims
Tires	Standard: 185/70 VR 15 Optionally: 205/55 VR 16
Drive train	Transaxle unit with engine in front, gearbox in the rear, bolted together in a rigid drive unit by means of a connecting tube Torsionally elastic (25 mm/1 in) drive shaft in four bearings, to gearbox in unit with differential, dual joint shafts with length compensation to the rear wheels
Clutch	Single-plate, dry clutch

Gearbox	Fully-synchronized manual gearbox at the rear axle, in one housing with differential, central shift lever on tunnel	
	Ratios:	
	1 gear/i = 3.6000	10/36
	2 gear/i = 2.1250	16/34
	3 gear/i = 1.4583	24/35
	4 gear/i = 1.0714	28/30
	5 gear/i = 0.8285	35/29
	Final drive/i = 3.8888	9/35
Engine	Four-cylinder, four-stroke inline engine, water cooled, belt-driven overhead camshaft, two balance shafts to control inertial masses	
Bore	100 mm	
Stroke	78.9 mm	
Capacity	2479 cc	
Compression ratio	10.6 : 1	
Engine output	120 kW DIN at 5800 rpm (163.2 HP)	
max. torque	205 Nm at 3000 rpm (20.9 kpm/151.2 lb-ft)	
Crankshaft	Forged steel, five main bearings	
Valve arrangement	Hanging in a row	
Valve drive	Overhead camshaft and hydraulic tappets	
Camshaft drive	By cogged belt	
Lubrication	Pressure lubrication with crescent pump	
Oil filter	In main stream	
Mixture preparation	Bosch L-Jetronic	
Fuel delivery	Electric fuel pump	
Octane requirement	98 RON/88 MON	

Electrical system	12 V 45 Ah battery 1260 Watt/90 A alternator	
Dimensions	Wheelbase	2400 mm/ 94.6 in
	Front track	1477 mm/ 58.2 in
	Rear track	1451 mm/ 57.2 in
	Length	4200 mm/165.5 in
	Width	1735 mm/ 68.4 in
	Height	1275 mm/ 50.2 in
Liquid capacities	Fuel tank approx.	62 l with 5 as reserve (16.4 gal,1.3 res)
	Engine oil	5.5 l/5.8 qt
	Engine cooling	7.0 l/7.4 qt
	Gearbox oil	2.6 l/2.8 qt
	Brake fluid reservoir	0.2 l/0.8 qt
	Windshield and headlight cleaner reservoir approx.	6.4 l/6.8 qt
Weights	DIN Empty weight	1180 kg/2600 lb
	Permit total weight	1500 kg/3310 lb
Performance	Acceleration 0–100 km/h (0–62 mph)	8.4 s
	Automatic gearbox	9.6 s
	1 km, standing start (0.62 miles)	29.0 s
	Top speed	220 km/h (137 mph)
Fuel consumption	7.0 l/100 (33.6 mpg) at 90 km/h (56 mph) 8.7 l/100 (27.0 mpg) at 120 km/h (75 mph) 11.4 l/100 (20.6 mpg) on city cycle	

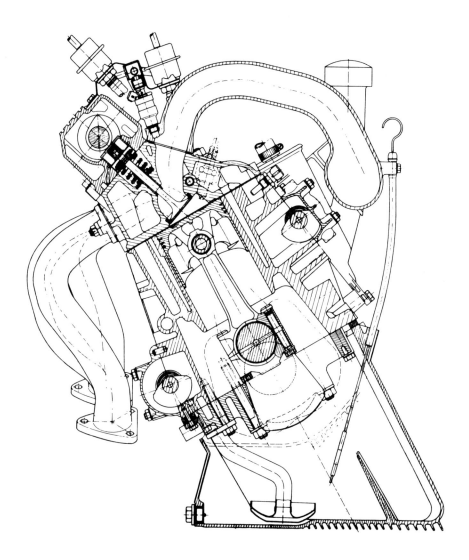

*Frontal elevation of the 944 engine. Note the wedge shaped combustion chambers and
staggered location of harmonic balancing shafts.*

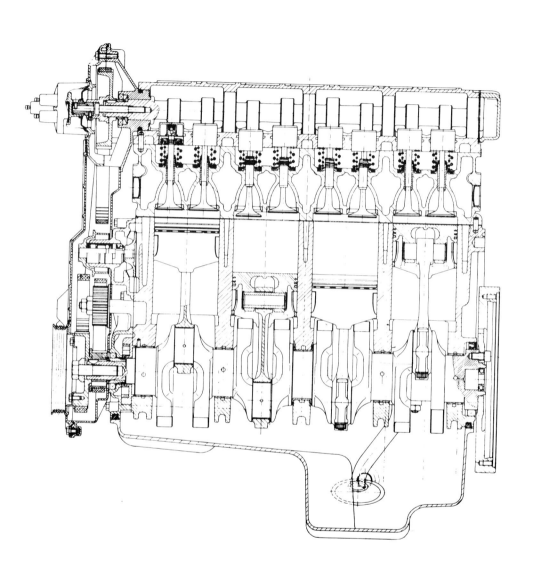

944 engine in technical drawing form in side elevation.

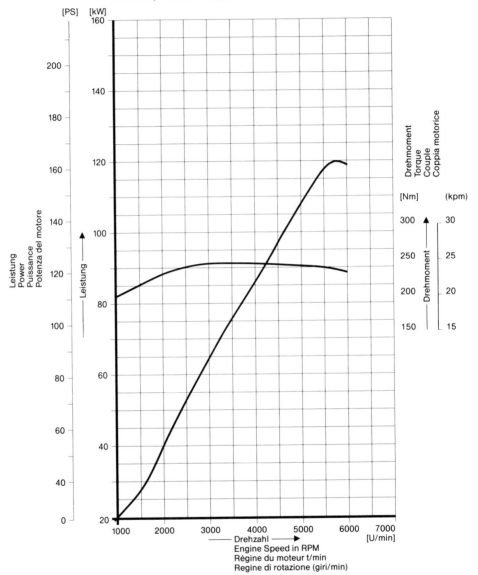

Leistung und Drehmoment des Porsche 944
Performance and torque of the Porsche 944
Puissance et couple de la Porsche 944
Curve di potenza e coppia motorice della Porsche 944

Porsche technical chart showing performance and torque curves. Note the extremely flat profile for the torque.

144

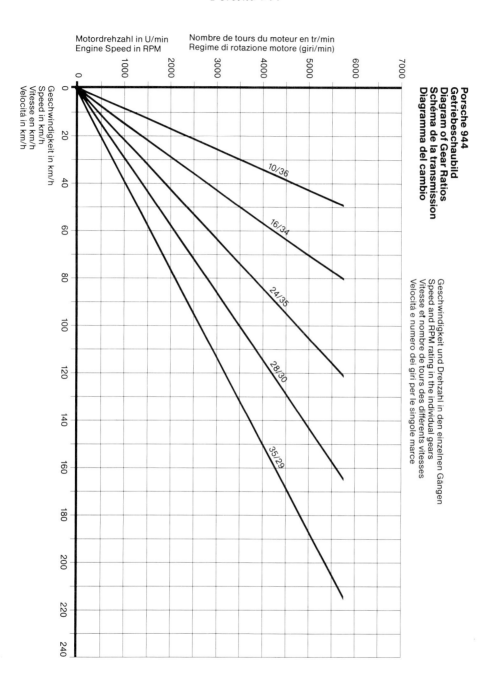

Porsche technical chart graphically demonstrating gear ratios.